Pagliacci has Nothing on Me!

Marguerite Piazza

with

Marguerite Bonnett

ISBN 978-1-84728-394-8
Printed in the United States of America.

Table of Contents

Part 5

Part 6

Dedication

This book is dedicated to my beautiful and brilliant
daughter, Marguerite, without whose talent and
dedication this book would not exist.
Love, Mama

Marguerite Piazza

Acknowledgements

Growing up the daughter of a celebrity put me in a unique position to observe an extraordinary life. When it came to excitement, interesting people, exotic places, sparkling events and a big noisy family who loved each other, my life was resplendent and truly blessed. With Marguerite Piazza for a mother, everything was a magnificent performance, from the Christmas mornings that made department store displays look dull to a simple family dinner. Whatever Mama does, she does it with style and flair and I am so grateful for all the many things and events and memories I will always hold dear.

As a child, I listened intently as Mama regaled friends and family alike with amazing stories of her adventures on and off the stage. I remember gasps of shock followed by howling laughter and a good time had by all. Thank you, Mama, for being so patient with me as I tried to write them all down, while continually asking for more.

I would also like to thank Claire Gerus for her patience and understanding during the editing process. Claire's constant vigilance during my quest to match stories with correct dates, places and a multitude of long forgotten, obscured or lost details was inspiring. Her talent for smoothing out the rough edges and helping me make a series of disjointed stories feel whole is a special gift.

To all my brothers and sisters who each contributed to this project in their own special way, Anna-Becky Redlich, Bill Condon, Shirley Condon, Gregory Condon and Robert Bergtholdt, I thank you. To Jimmy Condon, we miss you.

And finally, to my amazing husband, Dovell Bonnett, I am so grateful for your unending love, support and encouragement. This book would not be what it is without you.

Marguerite P. Bonnett

Introduction

Each one of us has a unique perspective on the people, places and events that fill our lives. No one can tell our story but us, much as biographers will try to "get it right." Today, as I contemplate a life filled with passion, drama, creativity, and a variety of experiences one can only hope to survive, I marvel at the amazing gifts I have had from life, and the personal passions that have run through it, seeing me through the best--and the worst--of times.

Back in the 1950s, the early days of television launched me into a lifelong career doing what I love most--singing. In many ways, I've been blessed. My life has been filled with all the glitz and glamour of opening nights, from the Metropolitan Opera to the Las Vegas strip. And all along the way, I've been surrounded by highly creative and intensely powerful people. Some would help me. Some would hurt me. Some would entertain me. But all of them would teach me valuable life lessons.

As a young woman, I was very ambitious. Whether my goal was to appear on TV, radio, opera or in nightclubs, I accomplished almost every one I set for myself, and a few I'd never even imagined. During my heyday, I was blessed with good looks and a talent for singing that commanded enormous sums of money--this at a time when the business community offered very few favors to women.

In those days, I tasted success in a big way, and it truly was a sweet life. But it wasn't all wine and roses. I had my share of trials and hardships--some even life-threatening. Looking back now, it seems as if everything I've ever wanted has been in jeopardy at one time or another.

I was fortunate that, early in life, I learned my first important lesson--that it isn't looks or talent or money that gets you through the tough times; it's character. I define "character" as "inner strength and self-discipline." Thanks to my training as a performer, I developed enough character to survive four marriages, six children, the

1

subsequent deaths of my husbands, a long struggle with cancer, and the loss of a child to suicide.

Character is not something you're born with; it's something you cultivate. I was able to develop incredible self-discipline because of my passion for singing. I had an intense desire to sing whenever I could, and my self-discipline became a huge factor in my success, both on and off the stage. I would do whatever it took in order to be able to sing, whenever and wherever I was needed.

Perfectionism is something I have borne as both a blessing and a curse. The fact that I possess an unwavering sense of perfectionism has defined my attitude towards my career. Obviously, this can become an impediment when others are rushing you into a decision, or when "perfect" circumstances just don't exist. When I was in college, I had a voice teacher who once told me, "Make everything you sing like a string of pearls. Each note should be as perfect as the next. Only then, when all those notes are strung together, will they become something beautiful."

Looking back, I see that my entire life has been an effort to create that perfect strand of pearls, one day at a time. Perfectionism for me was about keeping my focus on my desire to sing, thus creating beauty. Every note, every syllable, had to be perfect.

But the most important element underlying everything in my life is my faith. I've always held a deep, religious faith, and felt that I possessed a real and very personal connection with God. When life really stumps me and I ask God for assistance, I have faith that eventually--in God's good time--my answer will be delivered. And it always is.

The stories that follow are about what I saw, felt, and did throughout a life that amazes even me. Sometimes my memory colors the facts. Sometimes it clarifies them. But these are the "facts" based on my experiences with grand opera, celebrities, presidents, husbands, children, and the early days of television. Now sit back, relax, and enjoy my personal "Show of Shows."

Part One

My Big Italian Family

I was born in New Orleans, Louisiana, a thousand years ago, or so it seems, but I remember my childhood as if it were yesterday. I chose young, beautiful parents--my father, Albert William Luft, and my mother, Michaela Piazza.

My father's forebears, the Luft and Von Alt families, were from Hassenfarmstadt, Germany. The Von Alts were titled people, though I believe it was a military title. Young Albert was big and well built, and when he began to court my mother, all her siblings would pile around to check him out. In those days, if you wanted to court someone, you could only come over on official visiting days: Tuesdays, Thursdays and Sundays.

My mother succumbed to my father's charms and married him when she was only fifteen and my father, eighteen. Marriage was like a fantasy to my mother, and she had a big wedding with all the trimmings, complete with a horse-driven carriage.

I was born three years later. I still have memories of the tall, blond, handsome man who would put me atop his shoulders for a ride, a ceremony we both adored. When I was only four, my father was a victim of a terrible automobile accident, and his leg was badly crushed. When gangrene poisoning set in, doctors amputated his leg to the hip, hoping to save him. He died a few days later, not yet 25. My mother was devastated.

Even in death, my father would have a strong impact on my life. After he died, my mother became everything to me--she was my life. I was an only child, and although my mother had a large family, she had no competition in my eyes. My mother was almost like a possession to me, and I to her. We were so close, we even thought alike!

My mother took her maternal responsibilities seriously and actually nursed me for two years. Perhaps that was one reason I felt so bonded to her. As I grew older, I just couldn't let go of her. Even when I was a grown college girl, I would go and sit in her lap, an odd sight, since she was smaller than I.

As a child, I had very long curls, which my mother created by wrapping strands of my hair dipped in warm water around her finger. Because the curling process took an hour every morning before I went to school, my mother became the world's best storyteller, just to keep me entertained while she accomplished this task.

I found my mother simply delightful. Once when I was very ill with the flu, she took me into the living room, put on a record, and started to clown around, doing crazy ballet exercises. I didn't give in at first, but it was so funny, she got me to laugh. This was pretty standard for Ma, as I called her. She did crazy things like that all the time.

As I grew older, I found that Ma often liked to go out in search of something interesting to do. My two aunts affectionately called her "the street runner" and indulged her desire for entertainment. She was so energetic and full of life, she could do no wrong. Everybody loved her.

We Italians are very close, family-oriented people, and I was always surrounded by relatives. After my father's death, I spent most of my time with my mother's family, who had come from a little village in Sicily called Bisaquina.

My great-grandfather, Antonio Noto, or "Nonu," had been a soldier in the Italian army. I can still remember Nonu seated in a big chair in the main room of his house in New Orleans, where he would preside over the day's activities. He kept a bottle of red wine on the little table next to him, which he sipped from a glass all day long. His cane was always propped up against the other side of his "throne," and he took on a pope-like demeanor, greeting visitors solemnly as they practically groveled before him. If someone did something he didn't like, he'd whack them with his cane. He truly was in charge!

I liked Nonu because he would tell me wonderful stories about the old country, such as how his mother would loan money to the nobles in Sicily. In exchange, she would keep the borrowers' silks, tapestries, and beautiful silver pieces in a small room for collateral, much as pawnbrokers do today.

Nonu's mother was quite phobic about germs--she believed that people died because they were unclean. Therefore, she had her own

4

silverware: a cup, a plate, a bowl, a knife, a fork, and a spoon. When she finished eating, she would wash her utensils in clean water, dry them with a clean cloth, and put them all in her apron to carry around with her. She would not allow anyone to touch her utensils or drink out of her cup. Surprisingly, all this took place long before Madame Curie's discoveries about germs. Great-great-grandmother just had an intuition about it.

In his youth, Nonu had been tall, thin, and quite handsome. He was also an avid hunter, taking his hunting dog, Diana (after the Roman goddess and huntress of the forest) out almost daily into the Italian woods.

When he met the girl who would become my great-grandmother, a tiny, delicate, truly beautiful woman named Francesca La Bue, he lost his heart to her. They married, and in time gave birth to my grandmother, Alfonsia Noto, before they left for America, settling in New Orleans.

There, as a teenager, my grandmother met the young man who would be my grandfather. She and her fiancé, Louis Piazza, were married at the age of sixteen in a little church on Rampart Street.

Affectionately known as "Mama" and "Papa" by their offspring and even their neighbors, they were like two little peas in a pod. One never did anything without first consulting the other. Together, they opened a corner grocery, and later a drug store.

In those days, every store had a specialty. You had to go to the butcher for your meat, then the greengrocer for your vegetables, a fish seller for your seafood and so on. Mama and Papa opened their little neighborhood market and did quite well, but they worked very hard, spending long hours in the shop to provide for their growing family.

Mama was actually quite a merchant. During the war, she would buy a carload of sugar, gambling that it would go up in price in a few days. Then, when it did, she would sell it at a profit. She was so successful at this intuitive exercise; she was able to put my Uncle George through Law School at Loyola University. Mama was a real risk-taker, but her risks were usually well thought out.

Mama wasn't one to laze about in a bathrobe. Every morning, she and Papa were up early, bathed, dressed, cleaned the house, and were ready to leave for work when others were still waking up. Mama was so orderly, she even went so far as to iron the dishtowels!

This passion for perfectionism filtered down to me. When I was a child, we had no air conditioning and New Orleans was so hot that, by two in the afternoon, I was a mess. Mama would bring me inside and bathe me, redress me, and have me ready to go back out to play again at three each afternoon. How my grandmother did all she did, I'll never know, but she never looked tired or disheveled.

While life with Mama Piazza was my first encounter with perfectionism, I found later on that all my teachers would insist on perfection. Now, whether I'm washing dishes or singing an aria, the results have to be exactly right or I'm not satisfied.

In their day, Mama and Papa had a baby every year, eventually giving birth to ten children. First came George, then Margaret, who died at birth. Next came Toby, then Michaela (my mother), Joseph, Frances, Peter, a seminarian, my Aunt Ann, Patrick, who died as a baby, and Lucile, who died at four during a flu epidemic.

When I came along, my grandmother had seven grown children. All of these people, plus their wives and husbands, were my immediate family. My two aunts, Ann and Frances, were more like my sisters; especially Ann, who later traveled with me everywhere. Peter, my uncle, seemed always to be ill. When he contracted encephalitis, he reluctantly had to give up his dream of being a priest.

Mama and Papa were infinitely kind and sweet. They were also devout Catholics. They went to mass every morning, and Papa knew his bible backward and forward. Mama was always praying for something, usually for one of her children.

One of our favorite holidays was St. Joseph's Day, when Mama cooked non-stop for days, producing a variety of beautiful breads and delicious cookies and pastries. She made several different pastas, one stuffed with fish, others with meat or spinach. I also remember a wonderful, sweet tomato sauce she made, which I believe is also a Sicilian recipe, though you never see it in restaurants. On March 19th, all this food was put out in the dining room, and the doors to our house were open to anyone who wanted to eat. We would invite people from St. Vincent de Paul or the Little Sisters of the Poor to share in our bounty.

I particularly remember my Uncle George when I was a child. When my father died, Uncle George became my official guardian. He promised my father on his deathbed that he would take care of me and he kept his word. I have never had nicknames in my life, but Uncle George always addressed me as "Child." I don't think he ever called me Marguerite.

Uncle George Piazza was an attorney in New Orleans with an office in the Pere Marquette Building. As a little girl, I loved to go to visit him at his office. While there, I would pick up and admire a beautiful blue glass paperweight on his desk that held a certain fascination for me. Now that he's gone, it rests on my dressing table, where I see it every day. It reminds me of one of the truly great men in my life.

My grandparents spoke Italian at home, as did most of my aunts and uncles, but my mother wanted no part of her Italian heritage. It's a strange thing, but often the first generation born to a family of immigrants wants to drop everything that identifies them with the old country. They want to become Americans. My mother was totally an American and New Orleanean.

She once said to me, "One thing you must never do is marry an Italian, or an actor. They are too possessive and want to tell you what to do all the time. And you don't want any part of that." Right or wrong, that was the way she saw it.

Although I had Uncle George as a wonderful male role model while growing up, women (especially the women in my family) became the dominating influences in my young life. However, as it turned out, men have been my closest companions and have dominated my adult life. You won't hear much about my close girlfriends because there were very few of them. But those women who were close to me have been loyal and true.

Recently, I was sorting through the books in my library when I came across an old dictionary I used in college. I stopped, fascinated, when I saw that, at the top of the first page, "Marguerite Luft" was written. Below that was written, "Piazza-Kritz." Then, below that, was "McDonald," and then, "Mrs. William J. Condon." Then I wrote, "How about that!" But there was to be one more entry: Bergtholdt.

There is indeed a story after each one of those names. Did you think this book was going to be about music? Well, it is in a way. Music is what has helped me survive all my encounters with men and other challenges in my life.

A New Orleans Childhood

Like many celebrities, my public performances came early. In fact, I made my debut on the stage at the age of two years and four months. It was in the Haynes and Martin dancing school revue. I was one of a group of two and three year olds, and we delighted parents and friends with some dance steps and songs. I recall singing "We Are All Little Peaches in a Row" dressed in a peach-colored satin costume.

We also did a number dressed as cupids, wearing a wreath of silk flowers on our heads and a one-shouldered pair of silk rompers, and carrying a silver archer's bow and a sheath filled with silver arrows decorated with ribbons.

I have a group photo of myself with the other kids. Believe it or not, the whole experience made such a deep impression on me that I can still remember being picked up and placed on a platform to take that picture.

I was not much older when I had my first elocution recital, where I presented a poem called "My Dolly's Clothes." A few years later, at age six, I did my first solo toe dance. My mother was so enthusiastic about this performance that she actually paid to have scenery built for it! When the curtain opened, the audience saw a big silver box tied with a ribbon, right at center stage. Someone would open the box, and I'd emerge dressed as a silver bird in silver lame tights. I remember that the costume had two lame panels edged with teardrop sequins hanging down in front and back, and two panels that came out from the waist tied to my wrists to look like wings. What a sight I must have been!

When I was five, my mother married again, initiating the first unpleasant male relationship in my life. My stepfather, Ruben Breland, came courting my mother in a big, yellow Cord automobile with red leather upholstery and big chrome pipes running alongside the hood. It was gorgeous and enough to turn any girl's head.

I must say, the man was tall, dark, and handsome and my mother fell for him like a ton of bricks. Ruben was a painting contractor from a small Mississippi town. I'd had my mother all to myself for nearly two years, and suddenly here was a man clamoring for her attention.

My way of showing my feelings was to cut up one of my mother's beautiful silk negligees with its wide band of lace to make clothes for my dolls. Did I get in trouble for that! It's the only time I ever

8

remember my mother spanking me. I admit I was a little spoiled, but I put up with Ruben because I had no choice. After a while, I even relented and called him "Daddy."

When I was seven, he won a contract to paint an army installation in San Antonio, Texas and we moved there for about a year. Every Saturday morning, my mother would drop me off at the theater and pick me up in the afternoon. The morning show, sponsored by the Booster's Club, had a movie followed by a stage show with a live orchestra in the pit. We all sang songs along with the orchestra, following a bouncing ball on the screen.

One day, a lady sitting next to me leaned over and said, "You have a very nice voice, little girl." After a few songs, the orchestra leader announced that they were going to pick one little girl and one little boy to come up on stage and sing. The lady next to me immediately stood up and said, "I want you to come and get this little girl. She sings very well." The orchestra leader picked me up, carried me down the aisle, lifted me onto the stage, and asked me what I would like to sing. I told him I didn't want to sing, but I would dance. (I guess I was just not ready to start my singing career).

I'd always gone to Catholic schools, but when I was eight, my mother decided to send me away to Saint Scholastica Academy in Covington, Louisiana. It was a good school where they always kept us very busy. We all had to join the Four H Club, an organization that taught farmers' children various chores such as animal-tending and jam-making. Four H stood for "Head," "Hands," "Heart" and "Health." I learned more domestic tasks at school, where we were shown how to wash windows and sweep the floors, two of my least favorite tasks.

I did, however, take to the violin. In fact, I won a gold medal in the school competition. The nuns used to complain that I didn't practice enough, but I could play fairly well without trying too hard, and I knew I was not going to be a violinist. When I won first place anyway, the nuns were very upset, saying I should have practiced harder.

Today, it's easy to go to Covington from New Orleans. All you do is drive across Lake Pontchartrain on the 24-mile causeway bridge. But in those days, you had to drive all the way around the lake, which took the better part of a morning. My mother used to visit me regularly, but one Sunday morning she called to say that the car wasn't working and she would not be coming.

Well, I had a fit over the phone. "I hate this school," I complained. "They don't feed me. I live on air and water" (which was not true at all) "and I want to come home!"

Surprised at my outburst, my mother let me finish and then said, "I'll see what I can do." She immediately called my Uncle Joe, who always referred to me as "the baby." Today, "the baby" was in distress, so Uncle Joe went to the trouble of renting an automobile to drive both him and my mother to Covington to pick me up. But, by the time they arrived at three in the afternoon, I was having a wonderful time playing and didn't have time to see them.

There was a price to pay for my whimsical nature. My mother was so incensed, she refused to send me back the next year. However, I didn't really care. Boarding school wasn't for me. I really wanted to be at home.

I didn't have my first official singing lesson until I was nine years old. I was now back at our local school, and one day I was on the playground singing my heart out when one of the teachers called out to me. She told me I had a wonderful voice and called my mother to see if she could give me some lessons.

My mother's reply was, "No. This child is already taking dancing lessons, violin lessons, and she's a Brownie. She hardly has time to play."

Surprisingly, the woman insisted. "I won't charge you. Just let me give her a few lessons."

My mother agreed and this amazing woman taught me my first song, "Love's Old Sweet Song," which I performed at the local high school graduation that year. Not bad for a nine year old!

I was only eleven, the youngest in my class when I graduated from elementary school. Somehow, I had skipped two years, but it was the teachers' decision, not mine, to graduate me. They recognized that I was smart and could keep up with the older children, so they pushed me--often, too hard.

Today, I believe that being quick is not as good as being a little slower and having to really dig to understand something. As a child, there were certain things I missed, like the multiplication tables. Even now, I cannot multiply sums off the top of my head like others who have had this training.

Upon leaving elementary school, I entered the Mother of Perpetual Help Chapel and High School on Third Street and Prytania. That first year, I had a frightening experience. I walked the seven or eight blocks to school every day. There was a beautiful old wrought iron fence around the school property with an ornamental gate at the entrance.

One day, as I walked out of the gate, I saw a man in his car. He called to me, "Hello, little girl. Can you tell me how to get to Magazine Street?"

Proud to have been singled out by an adult for such information, I said "Oh, yes," and began walking towards the car as I spoke. Suddenly, as I looked into the car, I could see that the man was naked from the waist down! I gasped and took off running, stopping only when I was inside my house. Although I was relieved to be safe at home, no one was there, and I longed for someone to return to comfort me.

When Mama Piazza came in not long afterwards, I remember watching her take off her coat and hang it up. She pulled the long hatpins out of her hat and lifted it off her head. I still was in shock and could hardly speak. She looked over at me and said, "Marguerite, what's wrong with you?" I said I couldn't tell her. "What do you mean you can't tell me? What's the matter?"

By this time, I was crying and finally told her what happened. On went the hat as Mama grabbed me by the hand and said, "Come with me." We went back to the school and told the sisters what had happened. From that point on, there was always a policeman in front of the school. The same man actually came back and pulled his stunt a second time, and this time the girls ran to the policeman. They didn't catch him that time, but when he tried it a third time, they did.

When the man's court date came up, we were excited to learn that all of us were witnesses and had to go to court to testify against him. In the courtroom, I got up and quickly identified the man. The other two girls were less definite; so the court fined him $50 and let him go. Sadly, some things haven't changed much from that day to this.

On the brighter side was my high school experience, where I found a great friend and accomplice. My neighbor, Marshall Capburn, was a

11

terrific young man, and we had great fun throwing parties in my grandmother's parlor. She lived in a huge house with cavernous rooms and high ceilings, and we would spend all day Saturday decorating the place just to see how inventive we could be. We'd hang crepe paper from the picture molding to make big, colorful awnings and come up with other wildly imaginative ways to alter the house.

Once, we had a Tacky party. We covered egg crates with burlap and put cotton on both ends to make them look like bails of cotton, transforming the formal parlor into a riverfront scene. We spared nothing to have the biggest and the best parties on the block. Marshall and I would serve dainty finger sandwiches and punch, and we even had a three-piece jug band... all for about five dollars!

The jug band was great. One man played the washboard, one played the stand-up bass, which was really a string tied to a stick on a bucket, and the third played our piano. Things were a lot simpler in those days of no liquor or dope--we all just had a good time together.

The day it all stopped was the day we were to have the South Seas party. Mama had a lovely, big palmetto palm tree in the front yard, and we'd pulled all the dead fronds off it and tacked them onto the picture molding around the room. When she came home and saw all those dirty palm fronds on her nice clean walls, she had a fit, closing off our era of party-making at grandmother's house.

In those days, Sally Rand, the famous "fan dancer," was all the rage and I continued to take dance classes throughout high school. All of us wanted to be able to do a fan dance and we made big fans out of crepe paper and dressed in flesh-colored leotards to imitate her. But our instructor was less than impressed. She wanted us to put the same effort into learning classical movements and steps, rather than burlesque!

Learning to Sing

I graduated from high school a few weeks after my 15th birthday. I really wanted to go to college, but my stepfather was dead set against it, claiming that, "a girl's place is in the home." He tried to bribe me not to go to college by offering me an automobile of my own, which was uncommon for a young girl in those days.

About two months before the beginning of the fall semester, Ruben died in his sleep of a heart attack at the age of forty, leaving my mother once again a widow. She was shocked and saddened by his death, and I reached out to comfort her. But my focus soon became centered on my freshman year at Loyola, where I was to enter the School of Arts and Sciences.

The summer after my high school graduation, my mother decided to take voice lessons from Mr. Dunkley, an Englishman who had studied at the Royal Academy of Music. He took his profession quite seriously and Ma found there was a lot more involved than she'd imagined. The lessons really cut into her time.

One day, she decided to take me along to her lesson so we could learn a duet, but her real intention was for me to take over the lessons altogether. I had taken a few lessons previously from a professor Joseph Schram, who taught popular music. But by the standards of the Loyola Music School, this was hardly a voice lesson.

When Mr. Dunkley heard me sing, he said, "You're not going into Arts and Sciences. You're going into the Music Department as a voice major." I was delighted that he had recognized my abilities, and agreed to let him spend two months coaching me for the entrance exam and audition. Going through this preparation, I knew that I had found what I wanted to do with my life--sing.

I loved both singing and learning about music. There was a recital class every Wednesday, when I could actually get up before an audience and perform what I had learned. I had to learn a new song every week and was building a nice little repertoire. The very first classical song I learned was, "My Mother Bids Me Bind My Hair" by Franz Josef Haydn.

I also discovered that I loved being in front of an audience, and that I was good with the public. Even though I was still a kid, people always said I looked like a leading lady, not an ingénue.

Mr. Dunkley was a fabulous teacher. He knew that I was "going places," and helped me by giving me voice lessons twice a week. They were supposed to last for 45 minutes, but I was never out of there before two hours were up. He made me rehearse everything, including walking on stage, walking off stage, going up to the piano, bowing, and indicating to the pianist to begin.

You name it, we rehearsed it until I became absolutely professional. He once said to me, "You see this piano? It has music and junk all over it, doesn't it? So if there was dust all over it, it really wouldn't matter, would it?"

"No," I agreed.

He continued, "But what if it had nothing on it, and it was polished and looked wonderful for a concert on a stage. If there was a little glob of dirt on it, it would be very glaring, wouldn't it?"

"Oh, yes, it would," I said.

Finally, he got to the point. "Marguerite, that is how we are going to view every song you sing and every movement you make. Not like it's a crowded piano full of junk, but like it's a polished piano, which we can't have any dirt on, anywhere. There can be no imperfection in your walk, in your bow, in your attitude to the audience, in every note and in every word that you say. Every little thing must be so highly polished that it is perfection. Only then will it appear spontaneous."

Even as a young girl, I had had perfectionism in every aspect of my life. And now, it was being continued with my music.

We as parents tend to underestimate how important early childhood experiences can be to a child. I consider myself a case in point: to this day, I remember every detail of my first stage appearances down to the sequined fringes of my costume. From my earliest days onstage, I have always felt right at home as a performer. And thanks to mentors such as Mr. Dunkley, once I was up there, I underwent a transformation almost beyond my conscious control.

When I was married and had children, our nurse, Becky Franklin, once said to me, "Mama, you are a show pony. When the music starts, you prance!"

College and My First Singing Jobs

After starting college and finding acceptance and a little reassurance, I began to venture out into the public sector. I got my first job (and my Social Security card) singing in a little German restaurant called "Kolbs." It's still there on St. Charles Avenue, just across Canal Street from the French Quarter. I sang with a trio: I still remember Louis Kutner on cello, a very elderly man on piano and an Italian violinist, Joe Fazzio. Every night at 6 pm I would sit on the bandstand and sing things like "Rose Marie," "One Kiss," and "Il Baccio."

14

The repertoire was semi-classical, and I earned a little money singing while everyone ate dinner. I also did a local radio show called "Enjoy Life Down South with Jax Beer." Jax was the famous beer from New Orleans at the time. The show ran once a week for half an hour, featuring the popular French Quarter musician Pinky Vidokovitch and his orchestra, with Marguerite Luft (as I was still called) singing pop songs.

Jack Simpson, the producer, moved to New York a year later and became vice- president of one of the world's top ad agencies, Foote, Cohn and Belding. It was he who would later give me my first big job in radio in New York.

I sang at every opportunity, whether it was to sing from the balcony of the Pontalba apartments in the French Quarter to open the Spring Fiesta, or to be a guest artist with a symphony in one of the towns near New Orleans. I always said yes.

The engagement I remember most was a tour put together by my friend, Marshall, who always stirred things up. One day, he said, "I want you to do a tour for the Catholic USO." We were now at war and he insisted, "The men needed some entertainment at the army camps." The Navy was putting on one performance in New Orleans, one in Biloxi, Mississippi and one in Montgomery, Alabama. Marshall was an excellent sweet-talker--he actually convinced my mother to let me go. He told me, "You're gonna put on a whole recital, like a regular star."

And I did. At the show in New Orleans, I was introduced as a student from Loyola University. We had a Navy gob (a boy who played the piano) and a station wagon that Marshall convinced the Navy to loan us to get to the shows.

Although I was only 16 at the time and had never been to New York City, a small detail like that would never stop Marshall. When we arrived in Biloxi, he decided to get high-powered with the press there. Suddenly, I was Marguerite Luft, the "star from New York!" I always got a little nervous when Marshall did things like that, but somehow I always went along with him. I did the show, which everyone enjoyed, and came home.

The following week, we went to Montgomery, where Marshall had a great idea. "I'm going to get the governor to come to the program tonight."

15

I said, "Marshall, quit it. You're getting carried away now." But the more I admonished him, the deeper he plunged into his fantasy of getting the governor to watch me perform.

Now, he told me, "Watch this," picked up the telephone, and dialed the governor's office. He then proceeded to explain that a Broadway star was in town to do a show at the Catholic USO. Would the governor like to receive her? He told the governor's office that the mayor wanted to bring the young star over to him for a meeting at about three o'clock.

Well, if the mayor was going to bring her over, of course the governor would receive her. After Marshall finished speaking to the governor's office, he called the mayor's office and reported that the governor was expecting a star from Broadway to come over about three o'clock. Would the mayor like to escort her?

The mayor's office said, "The governor is expecting her?"

"Yes," Marshall confirmed.

"Well, then, the mayor would be delighted to escort her."

Honestly, Marshall would have been a stellar press agent! By the time the mayor came to get me, I was trembling. I thought surely I was going to be arrested for pretending to be something I was not.

To my amazement, everyone arrived dressed in evening clothes-- ball gowns and long white gloves--and the governor appeared in tails. The rest of the audience was made up of young boys in uniform. What a night! I still have the photographs of me standing on the Capitol steps with both the mayor and the governor. The event made all the local papers. Dear Marshall, what a gift he had to make things happen.

Following up on my previous night's performance, the next day I went to the Naval Hospital to visit the wounded soldiers. They were so excited to see me, it didn't matter who I was--I was young and pretty and I was giving them some attention.

While I was in college, I decided to try out for Loyola's cheerleading squad. To my delight, I was accepted. Mr. Dunkley wasn't happy about it, though, and warned that if I did too much yelling, I could ruin my voice.

When I refused to give it up, we made a deal. He told me I could remain a cheerleader on one condition: I couldn't yell. Instead, I would have to pantomime everything! I agreed, and for two years went through all the motions and gyrations like the other cheerleaders, only mouthing the words. Nobody ever knew the difference.

Marguerite Piazza in 1951

Papa and Mama Piazza

Marguerite with Her Mother

Part Two

Singer Available: From Mardi Gras Ball to Synagogue

When I was 16 years old and a freshman in college, I was named queen of the Virgilians' Society Ball. This event was different from every other Mardi Gras ball. While other groups simply presented their maids and the king and queen of their organization, who sat on a gilded throne, we Virgilians actually put on a show.

My Uncle George was the founder of the Virgilians' Society, a group of Italian professional men and women who decided to have a Carnival Ball. This was the first Virgilians Ball and the theme was Dante's Inferno. It was quite a production. There were five different scenes, all of which were elaborately staged. We were very proud of Uncle George, who played Dante.

The final scene after the presentation of the king and queen was a vision of Hell. The king looked like a devil with great black wings and I was Francesca da Rimini, dressed as a flame. My headdress resembled the head of a lit match. It was a red sequined skullcap that came to a helmeted point over my forehead, with great flames extending up from the cap in gold sequins tipped in red and orange.

The dress itself was a gold-sequined sheath with flames flying off the shoulders. The bottom edge was scalloped and cut up the front so my knees showed. When I walked, my whole leg came through. That outfit was absolutely gorgeous!

I carried a long, gold scepter with a flame made of red, gold and orange stones. The dress had long sleeves, and my back was bare down to the waist. It took several strong men to get frail, little me in that enormous costume into the auditorium. But I pulled it around all night long, bowing and smiling. By the time I got home at 5 am, I couldn't go to sleep; I still wanted to continue bowing and smiling like some sort of automaton.

I performed with a lot of orchestras from the surrounding towns in Louisiana, Mississippi and Alabama. In those days, there were fewer people aspiring to be entertainers, so when one appeared who was eager and available, he or she was sought after. I took advantage of all those opportunities. I always said yes, and that was an important step for me. I learned that you can't wait for a perfect walk-on moment. The only way to really learn is by doing.

While at Loyola, I was offered a job as soprano soloist at Temple Israel. I was part of a quartet, and during the summer each of us took a month to sing solo services while the others were off. When it came my turn, Rabbi Feibleman went to my teacher, Mr. Dunkley (who was the organist), and said, "This child is too young. She will never be able to sing the solo services." I was about 15 years old. But Mr. Dunkley convinced him to give me a chance.

That Saturday, I sang the solo services. After it was over, Rabbi Feiblemen came back to see me, kissed me on the cheek, and said, "It was wonderful. You can do all the rest." We became fast friends, and from that time until the day he died, he came to every performance I did in the city of New Orleans.

I sang a lot of religious music when I was very young. On Friday nights and Saturday mornings, I sang for the synagogue on St. Charles Avenue. On Wednesday nights and Sunday mornings, I sang for the Baptist services. On weeks that I didn't sing for the Baptists, I would sing either for the Unitarians or the Second Presbyterian Church. Then I went to Mass for myself.

Another performance I enjoyed doing while in college was a shortened version of the opera, *Carmen*. I sang the part of Michaela at the famous Court of Two Sisters restaurant in the French Quarter, which had been rented for the night. Frank Finnesy, a plumbing contractor, sang the part of Don Jose and Anita DeBend, a contralto from New Orleans, sang *Carmen*. Mary Scott, a piano teacher from Loyola, later told me, "Marguerite, you were wonderful. In fact, you look more like a Carmen than the star because you have the fire of Carmen."

It was a very sweet compliment from a dear old lady and an example of the constant encouragement I received while at Loyola.

Vincent Youmans

When I was a freshman at Loyola, Vincent Youmans came to New Orleans to spend the winter. He was an extraordinary composer of music for Broadway and the movies, writing such standards as "Tea for Two" and "I Want To Be Happy." He rented the Walmsley House (the former home of the mayor of New Orleans) on Calhoun Street, which was near both the music school and Mr. Dunkley's house.

To educate himself, Vincent studied orchestration with Mr. Dunkley, the head of both the music department and the voice department. Mr. Dunkley told him about me, and one day Vincent came to my singing lesson. He had been very sick with tuberculosis, but continued to burn the candle at both ends, which he would do throughout his career.

Vincent was very sweet to me; in fact, he "adopted" me for a while. He was writing a Spanish opera (hence the orchestration lessons), which to my knowledge was never produced. One afternoon, he took me to Werline's Music Store on Canal Street, where he bought every piece of his music they had in the store. Then, he presented it all to me. He said of all the songs he had written, his favorite was "Through the Years."

To my delight, he then took me to Mr. Dunkley's studio, where he played it while I sang it. In time, I sang all of his songs in that memorable studio.

Vincent Youmans was a composer who had melodies racing around inside his head. In the case of his current project, I found the opera he was composing very melodic. Although he didn't have any words for it, he would whistle the melody while he played the piano. I would listen, then "la-la-la" it. He wanted to hear what the voice would sound like on a particular phrase. It was a wonderful experience to be part of the creative process in action.

My contribution to music has always been to take a work of art from the written page and bring it to life. But to work with someone who was collecting this information in his head, and then seeing it written down on paper, was fascinating.

Sometimes, after working for hours, Vincent would say, "Let's go take a ride." We would get in his car and ride out to Lake Pontchartrain. Abutting that New Orleans lake are huge stone steps going down into the water. We would sit there and watch the waves while he told me stories about his life in New York.

He talked about all the things he did, the shows he'd produced, and how little he took care of himself. He said he drank a bottle of Scotch every day and stayed up till three or four in the morning. Then, he would get up early the next day to go out and play tennis after working such long hours.

Finally, his body simply couldn't take it all and he got sick. This, in fact, was why he was in New Orleans--to rest and recover.

I confided in him about my desire to go to New York to sing, to be a star. Even at age 15, I was very ambitious. But Vincent said, "You have to stay here and prepare yourself properly. If you go now and you're not prepared, you might just be a flash in the pan. Without knowledge behind what you are doing, you might not last. Stay here, get your degree and then go to New York and be an overnight success."

So that's what I did--and I did become an "overnight success" because I was prepared. I had all that knowledge and all those performances under my belt before I ever got to the big city.

Vincent had been right. Performance time is very important, and having to learn it, digest it, sing it and then perform it in recital before the whole music school was the best training I could have had. It had been very good advice for me to stay, and I was only 18 when I graduated from college.

Later, when I was doing graduate work, I spent one summer in New York with my teacher from LSU, and met with Vincent and his wife, "Boots." They took me out to dinner and we had a wonderful time catching up.

When I returned to New York to live, I called Vincent again, but he was too sick to go out and died shortly after that. A sweet, fascinating man, he'd been a tremendous influence in my development as a performer.

My First Boyfriend

My first serious boyfriend was Julius Roy Burgoyne. I was now seventeen, and we had dated for about a year when I decided I was going to marry him. Julius was the first intern in dentistry at Charity Hospital in New Orleans. He did a lot of surgery and consequently was considered one of the finest men in his field. He asked my Uncle George for my hand in marriage, and since everyone in the family liked Julius, we expected no objections.

We got as far as setting the date, ordering invitations, and purchasing the shoes. My mother had bought me china, glasses and silver. We were still looking for the dress.

22

Then, disaster struck. Julius' sister was married to a dentist who had gone away to war. When he returned, he began to make a big fuss over the fact that his wife was a Baptist and not a Catholic. I'm sure if he had asked, she would have converted in a second.

While he hadn't cared about that when he married her, now he used it as an excuse for a divorce. Julius's father was Catholic and his mother was Baptist. Nothing much was said about the Catholic Church in their house, so his mother took the children to her church.

When Julius' brother-in-law attacked the Baptist faith, the family was so devastated that it turned them against the Catholic faith. Clearly, his attack had nothing to do with the Catholic Church; it was actually (no surprise) all about another woman.

One evening, Julius came to me and said there was one thing we needed to discuss: if we ever had children, they would have to be brought up Baptist. I looked at him and said, "Yours will be Baptist and mine will be Catholic." And that was the end of that. Happily, we remained very good friends for decades. Clearly, we weren't meant to be husband and wife, but later he became the brother I had never had.

Graduate School

After four years, I graduated from Loyola with a Bachelor of Music degree. In fact, I still have my pink tassel in a box somewhere deep in my closet. I went to LSU (Louisiana State University) to work on my Masters Degree, and only lacked a few hours to attain it. I had chosen LSU because of the teacher, Pasquale Amato, head of the voice and opera department and Louis Hasselmans, conductor in residence.

Mr. Amato had been one of the great baritones at the time of Caruso at the Metropolitan Opera. He told me wonderful stories about Caruso and the things that had gone on when he was at the Met. Once, he said, Caruso thought it might be fun to switch rolls without telling anyone. This was possible because Caruso could sing baritone as well as tenor, while Amato could sing tenor as well as baritone.

One day, they did just that. They switched a few pieces of clothing, walked out on stage and sang each other's roles. An exuberant time was had by both of them!

I was delighted with these stories and eventually Mr. Amato and his wife became very close to me. They would have adopted me as their daughter if I had not had a family of my own.

My first real sense of an opera company came from LSU's Pasquale Amato and Louis Hasselmans. It was actually Hasselmans who told me, "When you enter a theater for a performance, you take your personality, like your coat, and hang it at the stage door. You must become the character you are playing."

I learned my lessons well, and performed my first *La Boheme* under the direction of these two great talents. I remember when we were staging the end of the last act, when Mimi dies, and I was on the bed lying on my back. Mr. Amato stopped the rehearsal, came over to me, picked me up by the waist (of course, I was a little slip of a thing) and turned me over on my side.

"You cannot sing lying flat on your back," he said. "You will lose support from the diaphragm. On your side, you can use your arm as a lever to lift yourself up and down and you will be in complete control, not only of your body, but your voice. This will also give you projection to the front."

Of course, that makes complete sense. *La Boheme* was a new and unique experience for me. We played eight nights and I sang Mimi one night and Musetta the next throughout the run.

My mother knew nothing about the stage, but possessed a wonderful balance of intuition and common sense. She was always telling me to sing to the front, not the wings, as my voice would be lost there. She also told me, "Be like a little bird. Sing! Project! Lily Pons will take a note, spin it out to the end and captivate the audience."

Lily Pons was a famous coloratura who everyone thought of as French. She was actually half French, but her mother was Italian and she spoke Italian at home. Around our house, we took great pleasure in recognizing that the "Little French Canary" was actually quite Italian.

At the end of my first year at LSU, Mr. and Mrs. Amato took me with them to New York. We had a lesson every day and Mr. Amato arranged for me to have an audition at the Met. He wanted me to go in looking like the teenager I was. I wore a red silk dress, white bobby socks and low-heeled pumps.

Walking onto the stage, I sang the powerful aria, "Pace Pace Mio Dio," dressed like a child. What was I doing? I wondered. This was a ridiculous choice of music, and I wasn't a dramatic soprano; I was a lyric soprano.

There were two other girls auditioning that day, and we were all about the same age. One girl was dressed in a black velvet suit with her hair piled stylishly on top of her head. She walked out on stage in her spiked heels and sang a coloratura aria, and I was impressed with how great she sounded. When she was chosen instead of me, I wasn't surprised. I was told that I had a wonderful voice, but that I should go home and grow up a little more and come back later.

The other girl was Patrice Munsel. After she was accepted, Sol Hurok took her on tour. He then dressed her in bobby socks with her hair down and a bow in it. I had known it was foolish to dress like a teenager for that audition, but I had been operating on the advice of my teacher.

I went home for a while, but it wasn't long before I was in New York to stay. Strangely enough, when I did make my debut at the Met as Rosalinda in *Die Fledermaus*, it was Patrice Munsel who sang the soubrette part of Adele!

I had a great time in New York that summer. My dear friend, Father Chapman, had friends there, and he insisted I call them. They were twins: Anna and Margaretha Bromer. Margaretha and I bonded immediately and I stayed with her almost every weekend that summer and for many weekends while I lived in New York. I later sang for her wedding at St. Patrick's Cathedral.

There was a young boy from Peru who was about my age named Edward Power. As Margaretha puts it, he came for dinner and stayed four years. He became her surrogate son. We were both very jealous of the other one and very aware of who got the most attention at any given moment.

For Christmas one year, I gave Margaretha a present with a card that read "From your FIRST adopted child and I surrender that to no one!" I guess some of the drama of the opera I was studying was beginning to rub off.

I returned to LSU for further studies, but there was another teacher there who was not quite as good as my previous one, so I left before finishing my degree. I went home to New Orleans, but soon convinced my mother to let me try my wings in the big city. I was off to New York City to become that predicted "overnight success."

Marguerite in Carmen – Age 15

Mardi Gras Ball – Age 16

Part Three

Early Performances

There was an article written about me when I was first starting out in New York City. New York Post columnist Leonard Lyons said I was wound so tight, I was like a spring waiting to be sprung.

I can't argue with that. Fresh out of college and a new arrival in New York City, I was more than ready to get my career started. I really had a streak of luck when Eddie Dowling, a friend of my mother's, set up an appointment for me to see an agent, Sheila Dilly. As it happened, my mother was with me in New York and took me to the interview.

Sheila was a good-looking woman with lots of red hair and a sparkling personality. I went to only one audition, but she must have seen something, because she signed me to play the lead in Rudolf Friml's operetta, *Rose Marie*, at the Chicago Opera House for the summer.

Things went so well, I did eight weeks there, after which they kept me on to sing Franz Lehar's operetta, *The Merry Widow,* for another six weeks.

Doing *Rose Marie* was quite an experience. It was my first really big, professional performance and I learned a great deal that summer about producers, performers and the politics that go on behind the scenes. The show was produced by the Shuberts, known in the industry for their ability to cut corners and save money. While I had the technical ability to play the lead, I was still a newcomer to the stage as far as any producer was concerned, and I was hardly being paid top dollar. But I loved singing, and I told myself that the money would come later.

For the part of Emile, Rose Marie's brother, they decided to hire a real Canadian. The young man had a natural accent and was perfect for the part, with one exception: he had never been on a stage before.

As the story goes, Rose Marie is in love with Jim, but her brother, Emile, has other ideas. There is a very rich old man who lives in the village whom Emile wants her to marry. But Rose Marie doesn't want any part of it. She and Jim must meet in secret to keep Emile from finding out.

The Chicago Opera House, like so many theaters, has a set of doors that allow you to go from the wings (backstage) into the audience without being detected. We used these a lot during the rehearsals and even during the shows at times. The good thing about them was, when you were not on stage, you could sit and watch the show from the viewpoint of the spectators.

Now, it was my first big opening night and I was exhilarated to be standing in the center of a stage the size of a football field, all by myself. The chorus had exited, and Rose Marie was going to seize the opportunity while she was alone to call Jim in the little house on the side of the mountain.

Right on cue, I sang out the "Indian Love Call" and pretended to wait for an answer... at which point, brother Emile is supposed to come rushing in and say, "Rose Marie, what are you doing? You're calling that Jim, aren't you?"

Well, nothing happened. So, I gave the call again. Again, nothing. My heart was suddenly pounding so hard I thought the audience would hear it over the impossible silence. I was absolutely petrified. I had no idea what to do, except pray.

And it must have worked, because all of the sudden Billy Kent walked on stage. He could see that I was in great distress and said, "Rose Marie, have you seen your brother, Emile?" And I looked at him and said, "No, have you seen Emile?"

Billy was a seasoned comic who had done the very first performance of the operetta, *Rose Marie*, back in the 1920s. Later, he became an alcoholic, and for a long time no one wanted to hire him. Then, in the interests of economy, the Shuberts offered him the chance to play his old part, and he was thrilled.

I was grateful he had taken the role because Billy, now sober, actually saved the show. He started to tell jokes and one-liners while I played it straight for the next five minutes. Have you any idea just how long five minutes can be? And can you guess where Emile was during that time? He was in the audience watching us, laughing and having a good old time! After that, they hired a real actor to play Emile.

About a year later I was doing another Rudolf Friml operetta called, *The Vagabond King,* in Dallas. The comedienne, Ada Lynn, came to me and said "Listen, Marguerite, do you want to go to dinner on our night off? I have this friend here and he has a friend with him."

I said, "Sure." My date turned out to be the son of the owner of the famous El Mocambo Club in Los Angeles. They picked me up at my hotel and we headed for the restaurant. I was sitting in the back seat with this young man when I launched into my story about the first show I had done in Chicago, where the young Canadian actor had failed to make his entrance. I described how a comedian named Billy Kent came out and started telling jokes, and how Billy had saved my life, for which I would be eternally grateful.

"Oh," my date said, suddenly revealing keen interest. "Could you tell me some more about Billy Kent? What do you know about him? What kind of a guy was he?"

I told him he was a very nice man, very kind and full of fun, but that was all I knew about him. Then I asked him why he was so interested in Billy Kent.

To my amazement, he said, "He was my father."

"What?" I gasped. "I thought your father owned the Mocambo."

"That's my stepfather," he clarified. "My mother divorced Billy Kent when I was a year old because he had become an alcoholic. I never really knew my father, so I just want to know what kind of guy he was."

This sort of miraculous serendipity happens to me a lot and always delights and amazes me. I was so happy to be able to tell him some positive things about his father. This is just one example of how I see God participating in my everyday life.

By now, I was beginning to feel more like a "seasoned performer." Each new job rewarded me with something money can't buy-- experience. The more experience I had, the more self-confidence I brought to each performance.

I went back to New York after fourteen weeks in Chicago and moved into the Three Arts Club, a girl's residence run by the Episcopalian Church. The Club was populated mostly by young women trying to make it in the entertainment field. We had to abide by very strict rules, such as being in by 10 pm. We had to get special permission ahead of time if we were going to be out until midnight. I think that, if not for the Three Arts Club, my mother would never have let me move to New York City.

Jack Simpson, the New Orleans producer of the radio show, "Enjoy Life Down South with Jax Beer," knew I was in New York, but he didn't know where. He was producing a radio show in New York that would feature a young boy and a young girl singer.

Jack had found the young boy, whose name was Robert Merrill. Now, he wanted me for the girl's role. He knew how to find me: he put out a call for girl singers and all the girl singers in New York showed up for the audition. Except for me, since I didn't know about audition calls yet.

As fate would have it, however, down the hall from me lived a young secretary at NBC. Although we didn't know each other, she had heard me singing in the Three Arts Club's big community bathroom, which boasted a row of shower stalls. When she learned that Jack Simpson was looking for a young singer from New Orleans, she called him to tell him about me.

Soon afterward, he called me, and when he told me how he had found me, I couldn't believe it. I never did get to meet the girl to thank her.

Jack immediately hired me to do a new radio show for the fall on an NBC national hook-up. Here I was, a kid from nowhere who had gotten this job because my friend from New Orleans was the producer.

It turned out to be a great experience for me. Sigmund Romberg himself was conducting the NBC orchestra. Romberg wrote many of the great operettas, and we performed all of his original music. The show aired once a week and lasted for 13 weeks.

While I have a great love and appreciation for grand opera, I also love operettas, as the music is usually lighter and more like Broadway show tunes. They also featured big songs that gave a singer an opportunity to showcase her voice, but, unlike opera, the story line was mostly spoken and acted out.

And there was always a comedian or two, as well as a dance sequence, in the operetta. When Georges Bizet first wrote the opera, *Carmen*, it was considered an "opera comique" or what we would call an "operetta," because performers spoke between the arias instead of singing. Later, Bizet wrote the *recitativo*, which is the music between the arias, and it was then re-classified as "grand opera."

Meeting Husband #1: Karl Kritz

One of my teachers in New York was an operatic stage director named Armando Agnini. Mr. Agnini sent me to study with a very talented conductor, Karl Kritz. Enter husband No. 1!

Take one very young, talented and sensitive girl who is willing to work hard and drop her into the hands of a Svengali, and there's bound to be trouble. Karl was extremely talented, but while he was coaching me, he fell in love with me. It was not because I was a pretty little girl; he fell in love with my talent. Karl was twenty years my senior, but to me he was a knight in shining armor.

Of course, hindsight makes everything clearer. At that age, I needed a father and I looked for one through marriage. It's strange how being in love makes you so blind. In reality, Karl was short, stocky and had no earthly goods to speak of. But the musical knowledge and sensitivity he gave me, and the desire and will to work with me was worth, perhaps, all the suffering he would later cause both me and himself.

Karl had a job directing Ermanno Wolf-Ferrari's most famous work, *The Secret of Suzanne,* for the Newark Opera Company, and Agnini hired me to sing the lead. This was a one-act opera with only three characters: a man, his wife and a mute servant.

Agnini played the mute servant himself. The opera was set in the nineteenth century, a time when it was an unforgivable sin for a woman to smoke. Suzanne's secret is that she loves to smoke. There is a beautiful aria extolling the joys of smoking during which Suzanne actually smokes a cigarette on stage. Never having handled a cigarette before, this was quite a hurdle for me to conquer. In those days there were no filters on cigarettes and when I lit it, a little sliver of tobacco came loose and lodged in my throat.

I wanted desperately to cough it up, but I had just started to sing the major aria, and to cough would have been a disaster. For the first time in my life, without knowing exactly what I was doing, I used my mind to put the cough on hold (along with the piece of tobacco in my throat) and sang as if there were no disturbance to my physical body. It was at that moment that I learned about the tremendous power of mind over matter. No one in the audience noticed that there was anything wrong except my mother, who had come up from New Orleans especially for the performance.

Up to this point in my career, I had been Marguerite Luft, my father's family name. My mother, grandparents, Uncle George, my aunts--all the Piazzas had come from my home town of New Orleans to see me in my first "New York" performance, even if it was across the river in New Jersey! They all met Mr. Agnini and spoke Italian with him. Afterwards, he turned to me and said, "You mean you're Italian? Well, you're not going by Luft anymore. You're going to use Piazza." And from that moment on, I was Marguerite Piazza.

After that performance, I continued to work with Karl, who became more amorous and more determined to have me every day he was with me. At first, I was not interested in his advances, especially when I learned he was divorced and had two children. But the more I put him off, the more determined he became.

Finally, several months later, I succumbed. I, too, am stubborn, having been born under the sign of Taurus the Bull. Once I commit myself to something, I become unchanging and totally loyal. My mother came to New York and begged me not to go through with the wedding.

She didn't mince words. "He's too old for you! What could you possibly want with him? It's like pinning an orchid on a pig!"

But I saw no flaws in my knight, and in the middle of all my mother's tears, I put on a red silk dress and married the man.

During my first few years in New York, there was a lot going on in my personal life. Marrying Karl Kritz turned out to be my first big mistake. Oh, he was the greatest lover in the world, kissing my hand, clicking his heels, all done with wonderful flair. But I think he knew after we married that it was wrong. And he had defied my mother to do it. She did everything she could to break it up, but I was stubborn and married him anyway.

There were foreshadowings, of course. Just before we married, we went to a New Year's Eve party in Bronxville given by my "adopted mother" Margaretha Bromer Miller. Her Aunt Freddie was very intuitive and used to read palms. That night, she read Karl's and immediately pointed out, "You've been married before."

Karl said, "Yes, that's true."

34

She went on to say, "I believe you have two children, the oldest of which is 12 or 13 and is not well." This was also true. Karl asked if he could speak to her privately and they left the room.

We found out later that he told her, "I am very much in love with Marguerite and I want to marry her. Should I do this?"

When Aunt Freddie said no, he asked why. She replied, "You are still too interested in your other family," which turned out to be true.

I would later remember the words of a former voice teacher I knew at the New Orleans Opera Company. One day, out of the blue, he said to me, "Marguerite, I want to give you a word of advice. Never fall in love with a teacher of yours."

Now, however, I was in love. I believed there was no one else in the world except Karl Kritz. To me, he was the finest teacher and the finest conductor--and he really was all that. But there were problems.

First, he did not have the right personality to get along in the United States. He had grown up and become successful in Austria and Germany. There, they promoted one according to one's talent and with tremendous tolerance for the superegos that were allowed to develop among the super-talented.

Karl had come to America because of the war. Here in the United States, however, you needed to be both talented and good with people in order to get ahead. But Karl did not want to be nice in order to further his career. He simply wanted to be recognized for his talents, and for his genius, just as he had been in Germany. Unfortunately for him, this attitude did not work in New York, and it made him very bitter.

Karl was a man filled with turmoil. He had been forced to leave his European home because he had, in a moment of courage, refused to give up his Jewish friends. Then one day, the Gestapo came after him. Fortunately, someone tipped him off and he left Berlin with just the clothes on his back and whatever money was in his pocket. He boarded a train that would take him out of Germany and had another scare when it stopped at the border.

The Gestapo was looking for him, and blocked the exits. Then, they came onto the train. Karl got up from his seat and ran to the front of the train. The front two cars were in Austria, not Germany, and he was able to escape, but it was all very traumatic for him and affected him deeply for the rest of his life.

35

The second problem was his low self-image. After I married him, Karl began to feel that he was a lodestone around the neck of his young, pretty, talented wife. The truth of the matter is, he probably was. But I didn't see that. All I could see was a man I absolutely worshiped--my teacher, my lover, and the future father of my children.

The third problem was, as the psychic had predicted, his ties with his former family. When I didn't get pregnant after three months of marriage, I thought something was wrong with me. I even went to the doctor to make sure. Shortly thereafter, I did get pregnant. I was thrilled. But to my surprise, Karl was completely turned off by the idea.

He firmly announced that he didn't want another child, as he already had two children by his first wife. Now, I would have to "get rid of" the coming baby. Up to this point, our lives had been nothing but romance and roses. Now, I was shocked to hear that the man I adored, and probably would have died for, wanted me to kill his unborn child.

My mother was with me when I got the news from Karl. I was in Washington D.C. on tour in the operetta, "Desert Song," and was having a hard time with the production. The baritone was having an affair with the dancer, who decided she wanted to be the star of the show instead of me.

The baritone did everything he could to make me look bad on the stage. I had to sing a high C during a love scene while he was holding me around the waist. One night when I went for the high note, he squeezed me very tightly to make me miss it. His effort failed, and when we came off that stage I said, "Mr. Stockwell, if you do that to me again or if you ever come too close to me again, I am going to hit you with everything I've got... on stage and in front of God and everybody. I warn you. Don't you ever do that to me again!"

During the next performance, he came near me. I lifted my hand and looked him straight in the eye as I sang. He backed off. I would have given him a swat, too, even if it did ruin the love scene.

Now, on top of troubles with my leading man, I was being told over the telephone that my beloved husband wanted me to have an abortion, which was against both the law at that time and my religion.

My mother screamed, "Do what? You will not!"

I agreed, "I certainly won't. I want this baby." But Karl didn't, and when I was barely two months pregnant, he left me to go back to his first wife and their children. However, our fates were meant to keep us tied, professionally if not personally. That year, I followed Karl to Central City, Colorado for the summer, despite being pregnant. They were doing the *Abduction from the Seraglio*, a very difficult Mozart opera. The lead soprano part requires a coloratura voice because there are lots of runs and trills and high notes.

Eleanor Steber, a coloratura soprano, was singing the part of Konstanze. Although I am a lyric soprano, Karl said he wanted me to be prepared to do it. I tried to tell him I was not really a coloratura and I was not really sure I should be doing it. But I was the understudy and we had to be prepared.

Karl and I were rehearsing one day in a stable that had been converted into a practice studio. He played the big aria, which is known for its vocal pyrotechnics, and I sang it with great ease. When I finished, he said, "You see. You had no trouble with that at all." And I agreed with him.

But then he told me he had just played it a tone up. I couldn't believe it. He said, "I wanted to show you that you would have no difficulty with the coloraturas. I played it a tone up without your knowing it and you did it fine. Now when you go to do it on stage in the original key, it will be a piece of cake."

It just so happened that Eleanor was passing this stable where we were practicing and she overheard me singing. She has perfect pitch, so she knew I was singing it a tone up and it threw her. She developed laryngitis and did not want to go on anymore. So I went on. She was larger than I, but because I was pregnant at the time, I fit in her costumes, and I sang the rest of the shows.

A little pottery place in Central City made an ashtray for me that summer. It's a square container with a picture of me as Konstanze painted in it and it lives on my piano in Memphis. During this time, Gypsy Rose Lee was vacationing in Central City and she had her little boy with her. We used to paint ceramics together during the day and I got to know her. She was a very warm and charming person, very intelligent and very well read and I am happy to have known her.

After that, I knew I had to return to New Orleans to heal from Karl's emotional abandonment and to prepare for the birth. So I went through the whole term without the husband who supposedly adored me. Fortunately, I was back in the bosom of my family, who showered me with love.

When I became really big with child, my mother would not let me out of the house during the day for fear that someone would see me in less than perfect shape. At night, she and I would walk up and down St. Charles Avenue for exercise.

Motherhood

My son, Gregory, was born on October 31, 1947 after a very difficult birth. He was a huge baby, weighing nine pounds, and his large head further complicated the birth. I should have had a Caesarian section, but I had an old-fashioned doctor who let me suffer. I was in labor for 24 hours with violent pains that lasted a minute, with only a minute in between them. My Aunt Frances, who was a registered nurse, stayed with me the whole time.

A few days earlier, my Uncle George had brought me some lovely, fresh pears just before I went into the hospital. Between pains towards the end, I said to my aunt, "Oh, Frances, look at the beautiful pears. Aren't they wonderful?"

She looked at me and said, "What pears?"

"The pears on the table there," I said. There were none, and when she realized I was hallucinating, she ran to get the doctor. That's when they finally gave me the spinal block and I was able to rest for an hour. Finally, they took the baby with forceps. The last thing I remember was someone saying, "Marguerite, he has a full head of black hair." Then I blacked out.

When I came to, my mother and Dora Mae Jacobs were leaning over the bed saying what a beautiful boy I had. "Where is he?" I moaned, eager to nurse him. Poor little Gregory had one very swollen black eye, two big cuts from the forceps and a great big knot on the top of his head. He looked like he'd been in battle! It was awful. I took one look at him and said, "Oh no, is this what I got?"

Meanwhile, everyone kept saying, "Isn't he beautiful?"

"No, he's not beautiful. He looks terrible," I said. Though I tried to nurse him, I felt as if a concrete mixer had hold of me. I just couldn't take it.

The doctor said, "Take that baby away and give him a bottle." Then he turned to my mother and said, "This child is not strong. She should have a nap every afternoon for the rest of her life." Funny, I haven't had that nap yet. And that little girl who wasn't very strong would become the workhorse of the entire family, adopting the motto, "Whatever it takes."

The birth was over, but the pain was not. About this time, I received a bouquet of roses from San Francisco, where Karl was working. The note read "Congratulations. Karl Kritz." Well, that did it. My mother could not get over his coldness and audacity. It was a wound in her heart until the day she died.

I was in a state of shock after the birth and remained that way for an entire week. I writhed in agony, could not look at light, and had to lie perfectly flat, without even a pillow behind me. No one realized how deeply in shock I was until I begged my mother to get another doctor.

The old doctor, I suppose in desperation, had ordered a blood transfusion for noon the next day. At 11 am, the new doctor, an internist, came in to examine me. He checked my chart and saw that a transfusion had been ordered and cancelled it. He said, "This girl is in such a state of shock, anything more will kill her."

The doctor saved my life. I was terribly anemic and he started giving me small injections of vitamins. In two days I was well enough to leave the hospital.

Karl and Butterfly

When I got home, I received a telegram from Emile Cooper, a conductor at the Metropolitan Opera in New York. He wanted to know if I would like to do Puccini's *Madame Butterfly* in Montreal in two months. I said yes. Although I did not know *Butterfly* and had never sung it, I knew I had to do it.

I had a lot of reasons not to do the role. First of all, the only part I knew was the "Un Bel Di Vedromo." More important, however, I was sick. In fact, the doctors made me stay home for another two weeks while my family nursed me back to health. When my strength returned, I suddenly realized I was now a single mother with a family to support. With New York beckoning me, I decided I had no choice but to leave my newborn son in the expert care of my mother to return to work.

39

I had been back in New York less than 24 hours when Karl walked back into our apartment on 86th Street and back into my life by announcing, "You have to learn Butterfly." I looked at him and said, "Yes, I do. I have six weeks."

Apparently, Karl had come back to me to teach me Butterfly. It was a big, big project and we worked on it every day. I studied and I worked, I worked and I studied. During the last two weeks, Dino Yannopoulos, a good friend and stage director at the Met, came every morning and we worked for two hours. Karl played, I sang, and Dino directed. I literally learned that opera in six weeks and then performed it with the company in Montreal.

It was bitterly cold outside His Majesty's Theatre in Montreal, with six feet of snow on the ground. A path had been shoveled to the stage door, making the snow about twelve feet high on either side. My Aunt Ann, from New Orleans, where it is practically tropical, kept asking me, "You had to do this? You had to come up here and bring us into this ice and snow?"

I just said, "Yes," grateful that my aunt was there, supporting me, even in extreme weather. My wonderful Aunt Ann--I don't know what I would have done without her. She traveled with me everywhere and I couldn't have paid someone to do for me the things she did for me. Her husband, my Uncle Will, let her take off with me all the time.

I usually tell people I had four mothers: my mother, my grandmother and my two aunts. They washed me, they dressed me, they answered my telephone and they read my mail! They sheltered me more than I needed, but they were always there for me.

Aunt Ann is a little bitty thing weighing about 98 pounds. When I was working in supper clubs and I came off the stage, Ann took me to my dressing room, pulled my sweat-soaked dress off me, wiped me down with a towel, aired out the dress, and prepared me for the second show.

When I did my clown routine, she set the table up and took care of all my costumes and props, which was a lot of hard work. Then, she went everywhere with me. I never had to eat alone in a restaurant because Ann was always there, through thick and thin, throughout my entire career. And for years, Ann was the one I could call and complain to about anything, knowing that she would not love me any less.

Back in Montreal, Ann dressed me for Puccini's *Madame Butterfly*. We had beautiful, authentic kimonos and an authentic obi, which my Aunt Ann went to a Japanese woman to learn how to tie. It is a very complicated thing to do. It's not just a sash that you tie around your waist. The tying of the obi is a ritual in Japan. Usually in a performance, you would have one that is already tied and fixed with hooks so you can just throw it on and run. But Ann tied it for the wedding outfit and the nightdress every evening.

We played Montreal for a week and got great reviews. Madame Donalda was the head of the Montreal Opera Company and left me with one very special memory: one night, she had a reception for us at her home. After all the guests were gone, she turned to her sister and said, "Now, let's count the silver."

I was standing right there, but I still wasn't sure I'd heard correctly. "Count the silver?" I asked hesitantly, not wanting to sound foolish.

"Oh, yes. We always count the silver before we go to bed."

The New York City Opera 1948-49

The New York City Opera was begun in 1943 at the request of New York mayor Fiorello La Guardia, who wanted to create a center for the progressive opera as a counterpart to the more traditional Metropolitan Opera Company. I auditioned for Mr. Lazlo Halasz, founder of the New York City Opera Company at the City Center, just behind Carnegie Hall.

I was the baby of the company when I made my debut as Neda in *Pagliacci*. Mr. Halasz himself was my prompter, with Julius Rudel conducting. Mr. Rudel, who emigrated from Vienna at the age of 17, was a very talented conductor as well as an important musical administrator for a variety of venues, and went on to work with many of the world's finest opera companies. However, in those days, we were both just getting started.

My first performance at the City Center as Neda had gone well, and when I came off the stage, Mr. Halasz threw his arms around me and kissed me. I felt wonderful and his response was what I expected. I was used to kissing everyone in my family hello and goodbye. I kissed my uncles and aunts, my grandfather, my mother.

Everyone loved me and petted me, and if I liked someone, I gave them a kiss. It was a mark of respect to me. But apparently Lazlo Halasz had different ideas.

I took my experience with the City Center very seriously, learning and performing all the hard parts. I sang both roles of *The Gypsy Baron, Amelia Goes to the Ball, The Marriage of Figaro, Don Giovanni, Pagliacci, Traviata* and more.

After my first year at the City Center, I went to Colorado for the summer. There is a festival that takes place in a little town outside of Denver called Central City. It was a bustling town during the Silver Rush. There's a little hotel called The Teller House that is still in operation. In that little hotel is a bar where on the floor is painted "The Face on the Bar Room Floor", the subject of a very popular poem around the turn of the last century.

When I returned to the City Center in New York for my second year, Mr. Halasz called me into his office to sign my new contract. I had been very happy there, even though Mr. Halasz was a terrible conductor. He made horrendous mistakes and if you weren't sure of what you were doing and followed his cues, you could sometimes come in at the wrong place. He was notorious for that, not just with me, but with everyone.

I walked into Mr. Halasz's office to sign that new contract full of enthusiasm, but before I could take a seat, the conductor began walking toward me. He looked me straight in the eyes as he slowly backed me up against the wall, where he rested his hand above my head.

I was stunned. What on earth was he doing? I had never given him cause to think I would invite such outrageous behavior from him. Then, he began to lean over as if he was going to kiss me. Well, I'd had enough! I placed my hands firmly on his chest and with all the strength I could muster, pushed him off me.

Obviously surprised, Mr. Halasz went flying across the room and fell to the floor. I don't think he had any doubt about how I felt about his unwanted attentions. Quickly, he got up and gained control of himself, and was suddenly very apologetic.

"I don't know what came over me," he said, sounding puzzled. "I'm a very happily married man."

"I'm sure you are, Mr. Halasz. Absolutely," I replied. We proceeded to sign the contract and nothing more was ever said about it. I was secretly grateful that he didn't fire me.

On April 11, 1949, I appeared on the cover of *Life* Magazine with six other costumed sopranos from the company surrounding Mr. Halasz. Inside, *Life* did a feature about the new upstart opera company. While everything looked congenial, the truth was that Mr. Halasz had decided to fix me, but good. For every show we did, we had a rehearsal, then the performance, and the next day a review of what we'd done the night before.

The whole cast assembled for these reviews, and invariably Mr. Halasz would begin with, "Piazza! Why did you ruin the second act last night?"

"What?" I would say.

"Why did you ruin the second act? You were all wrong." He was constantly picking on me. He pulled all kinds of stunts to embarrass me in front of the company, and it got so bad that toward the end of the season, I had decided to quit. In our final confrontation, I told him that if I never sang again, it would be better than being there and taking all of his constant insults.

It turned out that quitting was the best thing I could have done. After that, the Met became interested in me. If I had stayed at the City Center, my move to the Met might never have happened.

Life in Manhattan

When Karl and I split up, I kept the apartment, which was in an old mansion on 86th Street that had been converted. I had what used to be the mansion's living room with ten-foot ceilings, opulent moldings and beautiful rosewood cabinets. That old living room became my bedroom, living room, bath and kitchen. Like almost all of the other old mansions in Manhattan, it was eventually torn down to build a skyscraper.

When Gregory was four months old, Ann brought him to New York so Karl could see him. I thought maybe if he could see his son, he would change his mind and start acting like a father. Ann and Gregory arrived early one morning and Karl came over to the apartment about noon.

When Karl opened the door, the first words out of his mouth were, "Did you learn the second act of Traviata?" Not "Where is the baby? Is he here?" but "Did you practice? Did you learn it?"

I said, "Karl, Ann came with Gregory. He's here. Don't you want to see him?"

"Where is he?" he said. I pointed to the crib. He walked over and looked down at Gregory and said, "Oh, he's a nice boy. Now tell me, what have you practiced?" He never even picked his son up. That whole experience was really difficult for me, and my Aunt Ann was so furious, she could easily have killed him.

Gregory lived the first few years of his life in New Orleans with my mother and Aunt Frances. He had the best of everything. My mother became Gregory's mother. She changed her whole lifestyle to take care of this baby and absolutely adored him.

This was the woman who wore gloves and a big hat when she went out in the sun because of her gorgeous, lily-white skin. But suddenly, when that boy was two years old, she put on blue jeans, a cotton shirt and a bandana and took him fishing. She made sure that Gregory did all the things that a little boy should do.

When he graduated from kindergarten, he had a plaster cast made of his hand by a man who came to the school for just this purpose. That day, the teacher said to my mother, "Mrs. Breland, would you like to come up and be the first one to see if you can pick out Gregory's hand?"

She said yes, walked right up there and quickly pointed out Gregory's handprint. Everyone wanted to know how she knew it was Gregory's. She said, "I've washed that little hand and kissed it too many times not to know it."

I eventually moved to a wonderful two-story apartment on York Avenue on New York's Upper East Side. Downstairs we had a big living room, kitchen, dining room, two bedrooms, two baths and a small terrace. Upstairs was what I called the "Music Room," where I practiced on my piano. The room actually looked more like a library with lots of books. I also had a fold-out sofa in case I needed another bedroom.

Off the music room was a huge terrace where I used to have parties and barbeques, just as I had in the South. Because we were on the twelfth floor, I was paranoid about leaving my children with a nurse.

The small balcony downstairs was just outside the children's room, which filled me with fear that someone would fall off the balcony. So the first thing I did was to have a privet hedge hauled up the side of the building in four-foot long boxes to go around the balconies. Even so, when I came home from work in a taxi, I'd look at the balcony way up there and then I'd look down the alley to see if anybody had fallen.

Next, I had a wooden fence put up. Now, I had an outdoor patio with a hedge around it, and a six-foot fence that wouldn't let me see anything below. Did this make sense?

A Fateful Meeting

About this time, I met a gentleman in Chicago who was an Italian count. His name was Giovanni Cardelli and he was a great guy. His father was a count and his mother an heiress from Chicago. Giovanni produced the American premiere of Benjamin Britten's opera, *The Rape of Lucretia* at New York's Ziegfeld Theatre.

The opera was staged like a Greek play, with commentators in Greek dress on thrones on either side of the stage. One was called "the male chorus" and the other, "the female chorus."

The story follows a Romeo and Juliet plot. Lucretia is Roman and Tarquinias is Etruscan. Toward the end, when Tarquinias goes back to rape Lucretia, the male and female chorus sing about his condition, saying that he is hot and heavy with desire. They tell how he gets on his horse, plunges into the Tiber River and swims the horse across. Although he reaches Lucretia, we are never sure whether she gave in to him or not. In the end, she pines away for him and the play becomes a tragedy.

Lucia was a young girl in the story, and there was an older woman who played the nanny watching out for both Lucia and Lucretia.

Kitty Carlisle played Lucretia, the lead, and I played Lucia, the young girl. Georgio Tozzi, who became a very big star at the Met, played Tarquinias.

As Lucia, I sang in the garden. Giovanni bought me real orchids to play with while I sang. They were absolutely gorgeous and looked beautiful on the stage. He insisted on nothing fake on the stage, and made sure I had them for every performance.

We had a short run in Chicago and then took the show to New York for eight weeks, where it was a big success. At our opening night

45

party in New York on December 29, 1948, Giovanni's wife, Jacqueline, wore a hat shaped like a Greek helmet especially made for her by Brooks, the famous Chicago hat maker--a vision I'll always remember.

Happy As Larry

I had some wonderful friends in New York who were dying to play matchmaker with my career. They decided to throw a party so I could meet Leonard Sillman, who was producing a new musical play on Broadway. Since the part called for a young, sexy girl and I had a good figure and could sing, they thought I would be perfect for the part of the lead, the widow in *Happy As Larry*. It was the story of an Irish wake and had been a success in England as a play. Now, Leonard was bringing it to New York, with special music written for it. It would be presented to American audiences as a musical.

It was1949, and I had just finished *The Rape of Lucretia,* which had brought me lots of publicity. I also had a radio show on WOR that presented operettas and the occasional operatic aria, airing once a week.

My radio show featured a big orchestra with an American conductor, Emerson Buckley, who later conducted several recordings with Luciano Pavarotti and others. What I didn't know was that Leonard Sillman did not like the show because we rarely did any popular songs.

When my name came up to play Larry's widow, Leonard was pretty sure he didn't want any part of me, but he knew his friends wanted us to get acquainted. To show his resistance, he ignored me all through dinner.

After dinner, we were sitting around the living room when my host said, "Marguerite, I want you to try this red wine. It's really good." He poured me a glass, handed it to Leonard Sillman and said, rather transparently, "Leonard, please take this over to Marguerite."

Poor Sillman--he had no choice but to bring me the glass of wine. He reluctantly walked towards me, but just before he got there, he tripped, spilling the entire glass of red wine down the front of my new white dress. Now he had to speak to me!

After this unexpected icebreaker, we began chatting. Finally, he admitted, "You know, I just hate that show you do on WOR. I think it's awful."

I stood my ground, however, and replied, "But did you see me in *The Rape of Lucretia?*"

He looked perplexed and said, "You weren't in it."

"Begging your pardon, but I was," I told him firmly, explaining that I'd played Lucia, the young girl.

Well, he couldn't believe it. "That was you?" he said. Now, this was a completely different story. Not only had he seen the play, but he thought it was great!

As I smiled in appreciation, he turned to me and said, "You know, I'm producing this new show on Broadway. Come to think of it, you would be very good for the part of Larry's widow. Would you like to come and meet Burgess?"

This conversation took place on a Saturday night. That Monday, I met Burgess Meredith, who agreed that I'd be good for the part. Everyone knew I could sing, so I didn't even have to audition. The part was mine.

Burgess Meredith played the lead opposite me as the widow. Also in the cast were Gene Barry, who later played Bat Masterson and Irwin Corey, the mad professor. The groundbreaking artist, Alexander Calder, a good friend of Burgess, was on hand to help with the scenery. It was a very modern set, with Calder's mobiles everywhere.

During rehearsal one day, Calder drew a sketch of my face and shoulders. It was very modern and I considered it quite unflattering. When I showed it to my mother, she agreed and I threw it away. Alexander Calder is now considered one of the foremost artists of the 20th century, and that little sketch would be worth a lot of money today. I seriously regret throwing it away.

Leonard Sillman never seemed to have enough money, and we made a few mistakes with the show. First, we were "on the road" in Boston for only one week before bringing it to Broadway, which is hardly enough time to work out all the kinks. But a theater had become available and we had to take it then or not at all.

The second mistake was a last-minute change before opening night. The play featured a fabulous ballet sequence called, "The Three Graces." There were three female dancers, one black, one Chinese, and one white. All were dressed in flesh-colored tights topped with an elastic fishnet bodice, making them look almost naked.

The night before we opened in New York, the ballet was completely reworked, which I personally thought was a crazy thing to do. As it turned out, we all got rave reviews individually, but audiences did not care for the show itself. It was way ahead of its time.

I didn't mind—*Happy As Larry* had miraculously given me my entrée to a major TV show. Producer Max Liebman came to one of the three showings we had on Broadway and came backstage looking for me. He told me, "I loved it! Now listen, Marguerite. I'm doing this show for television and I want you to be the singing star. It will be called *Your Show of Shows*. Will you come over and sing for Sid Caesar?"

Would I say no? Soon afterwards, I went over to NBC and sang *Musetta's Waltz* from "La Boheme" for Sid Caesar, who said, "She's in!" Becoming part of *Your Show of Shows* was the biggest thing that ever happened to me. It was even bigger and more important than my work at the Met.

Early Television

Most people think TV didn't arrive until the 1950s. It's true, TV wasn't popular until then, but the technology was invented in the 1920s. When I was still a kid and spending the summer of 1938 in New York City, I was asked to do a Mother's Day show on TV. There were so few TV sets at the time that I considered the whole event to be of little importance. However, looking back on it, I got to participate in the leading edge of a new technology and contributed artistically to a new form of entertainment at its very birth. It was a very unique experience.

For this very early TV show, the producers dressed me in wool from head to toe in a plain Scottish peasant dress with an apron. I sang, "Songs My Mother Taught Me" by Dvorak. The studio was a tiny room filled with lights and a single camera, and it must have been 125 degrees in there. With the heat of those lights and wearing all that wool, I thought I would faint. But the show went off without a hitch. There was no filming and editing in those days. Everything was live. I was paid a whopping $5 for my first TV performance.

As a young adult, in 1949, I was asked to do a TV show called "Young Broadway" featuring two boys, two girls and a piano player. It was a half hour show and we all sang and danced. Max Showalter, a wonderful actor, wrote a lot of the songs we did. Since television was still quite "new", it was not without technical difficulties. For the first show, I wore a white crepe dress with sequined sleeves, which looked horrible on the screen. They had to adjust the camera to eliminate the bright white glare, which made my face look very dark. When I saw myself I thought, "That's the end of my TV career. They'll never have me back." But they did. I was on once a week for thirteen weeks and got paid $25 a show!

Your Show of Shows

I was very excited about the opportunity to appear on *Your Show of Shows*. It was the first hour and a half TV variety show ever. The first one aired on February 25, 1950 and over a period of four years, we gave 160 performances. That's about forty weeks a year. The Show had everything… comedy, music, dance, you name it. A whole lot of what has been done since is a copy of that show. They used to call it "The Weekly Miracle" and it really was. We had all new material each week and really pushed the envelope of what could be done at that time.

In the four years the show was on, I appeared on almost every show. I did take two weeks off to have a baby and another few weeks off to have another baby, but that was it.

Max Liebman loved opera and took quite a chance on me. Everyone told him operatic arias, as a regular thing on television, would never fly. They thought only tap dancing and popular music would work. But unlike most of the divas of the day, I was young and thin. I was also pretty, photographed well, and sang well. So Max decided, "We're going to do opera."

On the first show, we did a piece of original music written by Clay Warnick, one of the musical writers for the show. The piece was written for me to do with a chorus of dancers. I also sang *Musetta's Waltz*. In the beginning, for at least the first year, Max would only let me do Puccini and Verdi because it was "safe" material.

Later, when we were more confident, we began doing other things like Mozart and even some operettas like *The Queen's Lace*

Handkerchief and *The Gypsy Baron*. We sometimes did a very short version of a whole operetta. Clay Warnick would cut the entire thing down to about ten minutes. We did a little piece of this aria and a little piece of that, plus a little bit of the dance. Occasionally in rehearsal, if it was too long, we would have to cut it again. The most important thing in our format was to fit the time slot we had and get as much of the recognizable music in as possible.

When I accepted a slot on *Your Show of Shows*, I really had no idea what I was getting myself into. It just turned out to be one great piece of luck. Thanks to the power of television, I was suddenly famous, even better known than other opera singers in the world. And as cable's reach grew, we acquired more and more viewers.

Doing the show required a lot of work and was extremely time-consuming. For example, Wednesday night I stayed up all night to memorize my lines. On Thursday, we were on our feet in the studio, blocking our moves. That meant we had to have memorized our material the day before. On Fridays, we had costume fittings. And on Saturday, we had dress rehearsal all day long, and then did the show at nine o'clock that night. We had to be in the studio on Saturday morning at 8am, and I was usually there till almost midnight. Multiply this by every week for four years…it was quite a demanding schedule!

There were a few exceptions to this, like the time I sang *Die Fledermaus* at the Met one Saturday afternoon. I went to our theater early that morning to rehearse for *Your Show of Shows*, then left to go over to the old Metropolitan Opera House to sing an opera, which was broadcast on radio, then came back and did the TV show live that night.

That's right. I'd done an entire opera for the Met and then a TV show, all in one day! And it was Fledermaus! The next day, I was sick. Come to think of it, I was sick a lot on Sundays.

Every week, we had a guest MC who appeared throughout the show to introduce all the sketches. They were usually other TV stars or from Broadway or occasionally a movie star. When we could not get someone for the show, Max would say, "Marguerite, you're going to MC the show next week." So, besides singing, I was also a part-time MC.

I remember one particular week when I was going to sing with a symphony in West Virginia. This was on my own time, but when Max found out about it, he had a fit. He did not want me to go out of town or to do anything but *Your Show of Shows.* The one exception was the Met. Max was very jealous of that sort of thing and always gave me a hard time about it.

When he found out about West Virginia, he said to me, "You are going to sing *Clavelitos* for the show on Saturday."

I said, "But Max, I don't know *Clavalitos* and I don't know Spanish. And there are a million verses." But he insisted I was to do *Clavalitos.*

I went to West Virginia on Sunday and was back on Tuesday. Wednesday, I had to learn this new piece of music. It is one of the most difficult things I have ever had to learn. It's very pizzicato, full of short, fast syllables.

Spitting out all that Spanish so quickly was not an easy task. There were no cue cards and there was no teleprompter, not that I could have seen them anyway, blind as I am. And to make things worse, I had to dance at the same time. But I learned it and I made it all the way through.

After the show, Max came back stage and said, "Well, Piazza, you did it."

I looked at him and said, "What did you expect?" What a taskmaster he was!

I remember another time when the MC couldn't make the show, and Max said I would have to pinch-hit for him. I had already agreed to make a special appearance at the West Point Sesquicentennial Celebration Saturday night during the show. I had arranged for a car to take me from the studio door to Carnegie Hall (about six blocks away) and back again to finish the show. I had rehearsed with the West Point Cadet Orchestra and felt we were ready to go.

But when Max found out about West Point, he decided to make me MC the show that week. I quickly realized that this was a power play by my boss and immediately resisted his intention to make me cancel my earlier plans.

"I can't, Max," I told him evenly. "Don't you remember? I'm expected at Carnegie Hall to sing with the West Point Cadets."

But Max wouldn't hear of it. His chin jutting out, he stubbornly replied, "That's the way it is, Marguerite. You can tell them that you can't come."

"I can't do that," I shot back. "I'm on the program and it's going to be broadcast on radio." I was determined to hold firm, even though I could see that Max was very angry with me.

I finally managed to meet both commitments by MC'ing the first couple of guests, then singing my bit, after which I'd run out of the building, hop into the limo, and be driven from Columbus Circle to Carnegie Hall. I jumped out of the limo, ran onstage, sang what I had to sing with the West Point orchestra, ran back and jumped in the car, and raced back to the *Show of Shows*, where I ran out on the stage to MC the next number!

I still can't believe I left in the middle of the broadcast! I pulled it off, but the next day I was sick again. This time I had a high fever. It was all just too much stress for me, but I did it and now I have the Sesquicentennial medal from West Point to prove it.

Besides being a lot of hard work, I really enjoyed working on *Your Show of Shows*. I was surrounded by great talent and wonderful people. The comics were very funny: Carl Reiner and Howie Morris were our regular comedic geniuses. A lot of people who are now very successful got their start on this show, such as Mel Brooks and Woody Allen. My good friend, Bill Hayes, who is still immensely popular from "Days of our Lives," was also a regular and used to sing with me on the show.

Inevitably, we all found ourselves jammed into one tiny makeup room. While everyone was fixing their faces, Carl and Howie would be carrying on something fierce, keeping everyone rolling on the floor laughing. More than once I thought if they didn't quit their shenanigans, I wouldn't be able to sing because my sides were hurting so much from laughter.

Sid Caesar and Imogene Coca were both comic geniuses. Max was always promoting Sid because he had helped him get started in the business. Imogene, on the other hand, was slightly older than Sid and had been around Broadway for some time. Before *Your Show of Shows*, Sid and Imogene had had a half-hour show on TV which lasted for 13 weeks. It was then that Max decided to create a show that would give them more air time--one that was an hour and a half long.

Imogene was actually very quiet when she wasn't performing. And Sid was, at that time, addicted to barbiturates and drank a lot. Once, I had a dinner party for him at a big restaurant in New York City. To everyone's disappointment, however, he just sat at the end of the table, drank a whole bottle of scotch, and didn't say a word to anybody.

Now, he has changed and has admitted to the media that he had a problem years ago. He's also shared how he was able to overcome it. He came to my house in Memphis a few years back when he was doing a play there, and we ate lunch in my backyard. It was a beautiful spring day and we talked all afternoon. Sid told me all about how he got rid of his addictions. Sid is a kind, sensitive, funny and wonderful man.

Jimmy Starbuck was not only the choreographer for *Your Show of Shows,* he was also my good friend. Jimmy was a fabulous dancer, having performed with the Ballet Russe de Monte Carlo and with some of the greatest dancers in the world. He staged everything from Imogene's dances to my operettas, and occasionally performed as well. I later hired him to stage a few numbers for me, including the *Pagliacci* routine in my third supper club act, and always considered him a brilliant talent.

All good things must end, and it was Imogene who eventually broke up the show. It was all about equal pay. When Imogene learned that Sid was getting paid almost twice what she was making, with both doing the same amount of work, she asked for pay parity. For four long years, she asked for, but never got it. Finally, she gave up and left the show.

During the last performance of *Your Show of Shows*, we were in the old theater at Columbus Circle, which we had used for four years as a studio. Television was still so new there were almost no professional sound stages, so everybody used theaters.

While performing, I noticed there were some men waiting in the wings for the show to end. They were there to demolish the building! The minute the show was over, they came in swinging with their hammers and claws. I actually said to one man, "You could at least let us change our clothes!" Later, a big convention center was put up to replace the old Columbus Circle Theatre. It's still there today.

After 1954 and the end of *Your Show of Shows,* my career took a new direction. I left the world of television and opera for the stage and popular music. But during the four years I was on TV, I divorced Karl, married Graves, had a second child, buried Graves, married again, had a third child and never stopped performing. Life was never dull!

MGM Screen Test

After I had been on *Your Show of Shows* for two years, I was invited to Hollywood for a screen test with MGM and was paired with Raymond Burr for a reading from a Broadway show. At the time, he was thin and quite handsome. The studio spent $5,000 on the test, which may sound like nothing today, but it had never been done before. I had everything going for me: a full crew, a beautiful set, everything. In fact, at the end of the test, I had a caterer bring in food and drinks for the whole crew, so everyone would remember the test.

To my delight, I was awarded a contract to do a movie with Mario Lanza. However, in those days there was competition between television and film. No one mixed the two--television stars didn't appear in movies, and vice versa.

To protect myself, I wrote into the contract that I would not give up *Your Show of Shows.* As a result, I lost the movie contract because I was afraid to risk becoming just another kid on the lot, when I was already a star on TV. Doretta Morrow did the picture instead of me, and it was Mario Lanza's only flop. So I went back to television.

Dave Garroway

In addition to being the first host of the *Today Show* on NBC, Dave Garroway had an hour-long variety show called *Garroway At Large.* The week I was scheduled as a guest star, everybody kept teasing me by calling me "Pizza Pie" and Marguerite "Pizza" during rehearsals. I finally said, "Y'all better quit that because you're liable to do it on the show." They said, "Oh, don't be ridiculous." The opening shot was of me in a beautiful dress and Dave Garroway's voice announcing, "Ladies and Gentlemen, our guest tonight is the lovely Marguerite Pizza!"

Of course, my face fell and he spent the rest of the show apologizing for calling me Pizza. Again, this was live TV, where there was no correcting your mistakes. Whatever you said or did went out over the air and there was no getting it back. It was a long time before I heard the end of that one. Earl Wilson even put it in his column.

A few years later when I was doing my supper club act at the Hotel Pierre in New York, Dave Garroway brought me a huge tin of caviar. As a result, my Aunt Ann and I didn't go out to dinner for days but stayed in my suite with lemons and crackers, eating caviar.

In 1951, Dave Garroway and I co-hosted the big Easter Show on NBC. I was famous for the hats I wore and always had one or two new ones made every year for the Easter Parade down Fifth Avenue. The NBC cameras were set up on the balcony of the Plaza Hotel and stars would stop by to say hello and make an appearance on the show. There was Janet Leigh, Arlene Dahl and Fernando Lamas, Jose Ferrer, Sid Caesar with his entire family and Al Capp, who wrote Lil Abner. The stream of luminaries seemed endless.

That year, I wore a special Easter bonnet shaped like an Easter lily. It had been made by the two little old ladies who used to make all the headdresses for the Ziegfeld Follies. They came out of retirement to make this hat for me. It fit on my head like a skullcap with a huge, hand-painted lily coming out of the top. It was fashioned out of white satin with two big yellow stamen, and it was a gorgeous piece of work. Its big stem was wrapped in brown nylon that came down from the hat to a white satin purse that had been made to look like a flowerpot. The purse had a little handle and a ruffle around the edge with brown nylon for the dirt.

I also had a lot of hats made for me by John Fredericks, who was really two people, Mr. John and Mr. Fred. Fred was my close friend, and we both had a ball with my hats. One of the first wild ones was created just after the flying saucers were in the news in the early 1950's. John made a skullcap of brown felt, trimmed with green velvet. It had about five tall wire corkscrews covered with thread coming out of the top. At the end of each corkscrew was a little round disk with brown felt on the outside and green velvet on the inside. As I walked, those antennae bopped around on my head. That hat made a big splash in all the New York papers!

Another year, I had the 'Piazza Parasol' hat. It was a bright pink skullcap, and on top of that was a real little umbrella with pink inside it and black lace on top. The hat had a handle that came down the side, which I could hold. And from its origins at the top of the umbrella, there were beautiful roses in silk.

My son Jimmy, who was almost a year old, was all decked out in a bunny suit, complete with ears and cottontail. He was crawling around under the feet of the cameramen, and every once in a while they would focus the camera on him. He was so cute that, for years afterwards, whenever I went shopping in New York, people would ask me "How is that little boy in the bunny suit?" As Andy Warhol would say, that experience was Jimmy's "fifteen minutes of fame."

My Most Embarrassing Moment

I was in Boston for a concert in the early 1950's when I was asked by the mayor to do a special performance for the Italian Navy, which was sailing into Boston harbor. My singing the role of Mimi in *La Boheme* was deemed to be the perfect welcoming gift, and I agreed to do the performance.

Everyone in the cast had performed this very popular opera many times. But when we went to rehearse, I was distressed to find that we had one lazy tenor. The man did not want to have a full dress rehearsal with all the costumes and props. He said, "We all know this opera backwards and forwards. Why don't we just run through it with the orchestra and be done with it?" Unfortunately, everyone except me agreed. It was against my better judgment, but I seemed to be the only one who disagreed with him.

Sure enough, on the night of the performance, the house was packed with Italian sailors, with all the officers in their fabulous uniforms in the front rows. The first two acts went splendidly and our demanding Italian audience was generous with its applause.

Finally, at the end of the third act, Mimi (played by yours truly) dies. Her lover, Rodolfo, is standing at the window staring outside. At this point, there wasn't a dry eye in the house. Marcello walks over to tell Rodolfo that Mimi is dead, putting a hand on his shoulder and saying, "Couragio!" Have courage!

Rodolfo realizes that Mimi is dead and rushes over to her bedside and, crying "Mimi! Mimi!" flings himself across the bed, dramatically ending this glorious opera.

What we didn't know was that the bed was on rollers. We went sailing across the stage, and I didn't know if we were headed for the wings or the orchestra pit and couldn't look up because I was supposed to be dead. It was awful! Instead of crying, the audience was screaming with laughter. Afterwards, they all came backstage and rather than hearing, "Marguerite, it was beautiful," I heard "Oh, Marguerite, that was so funny!"

At the time, that was one of the most embarrassing moments of my life. But it has since become one of my favorite stories to tell.

Husband #2: Graves McDonald

I was separated from Karl Kritz and had filed for divorce when I joined *Your Show of Shows*. During our first summer break, I went to Memphis to play *Rose Marie* at the Overton Park Shell for the Memphis Opera Theater. My friend, Ada Lynn (the comedienne in the show) and I went shopping that afternoon at Goldsmith's, the big department store in Memphis.

There we met the owners who gave us a tour and introduced us to one of the customers, a Mrs. Sally Smith. She was very sweet and asked us if, on our night off, we would like to come to her house for a barbeque. We thought that would just be great. There really is nothing like Southern hospitality. So, Ada Lynn and I went to Mrs. Smith's house on the Parkway. Her young son, Fred Smith, would later become Memphis' famous son, the founder and CEO of FedEx.

That evening, Mrs. Smith introduced us to two very charming young men, Fred Goldsmith and Graves McDonald. From that moment on, Graves never left my side.

When I left Memphis, I flew to St. Louis to do a Rogers and Hammerstein concert for Dick Rogers, who was a great friend. He wrote the album notes on the back of the jacket when I made my first recording, *Memorable Moments of Music*.

He was such a wonderful man. I had done the first Rogers and Hammerstein concert at Lewisohn Stadium in New York City. It was the first time they put together a concert of their songs and Richard Rogers conducted it. Now, Dick had taken his concert to St. Louis to help bail out the symphony, which is exactly what we did.

I was around a lot when Dick was working on 'The King and I' and he told me he was writing the part of the young girl for me. Because of the timing, I had to choose between 'The King and I' on Broadway and making my debut at the Met. I was really torn. But The Met was something I had longed to do since I was a student in college.

Since I had already promised Dick I would do "The King and I," I went to him and asked him what I should do. He said to me, "Marguerite, as much as I want you in the show, I think it's best for you to go to the Met." And that's what I did, with his blessing.

Graves McDonald followed me to St. Louis and stayed for the entire week, which I thought was very sweet. Shortly after that, I had planned to take a cruise. It would be the first vacation I had paid for myself. Gregory was three years old and I took him with me. Graves was supposed to join us on the cruise, but he failed to show up. That really upset and somewhat confused me. I couldn't understand why there was no cable, no call, nothing. So Gregory and I had a lovely cruise by ourselves.

When I returned home, Graves finally called and apologized profusely. I accepted his apology without too much question and we began dating in earnest.

During the second season of *Your Show of Shows*, my divorce from Karl became final and the very next day, in a whirlwind of romance, I married Graves McDonald. We flew to Mexico for the ceremony where Graves' friend, the famous and beloved race car driver, José Menocal, was our best man. José died tragically in November, 1951 in the grueling cross-country Carera Panamericana Marathon Race through Mexico. He was so loved by the people of Mexico that they tried (but failed) to abolish the race that killed him.

To divorce Karl and the next day marry Graves McDonald was a bit like jumping out of the frying pan and into the fire. Actually, I had no idea that Graves was an alcoholic. Whenever I saw him, he seemed just fine--in fact, he was wonderful. To me, he epitomized everything that was wonderful about men and about America.

At only 38 years old, he appeared strong and successful, but my impressions were based on occasional encounters. I hadn't really known him long enough. I guess I was always in search of my father, who had left me through death when I was a baby. I was always looking for that image in a man, someone I could depend on. When I met Graves, he looked like the Rock of Gibraltar and the Bank of America all rolled into one!

But that was far from reality. He could not stand the thought of responsibility. When we got back to Memphis after the wedding, I discovered he had already handed his business dealings over to his brothers. I made the unfortunate assumption that it was because he simply lacked interest in business.

After we married, Graves McDonald's aversion to responsibility became very hard on me. The thought of having a child to take care of was almost more than he could stand. When I told him I was pregnant, he wanted me to have an abortion. Of course, that did not sit well with me at all. Here I go again, I thought. How could this happen to me twice?

Then, Graves disappeared in New York and was gone for nearly two weeks. I had no idea where he was or whether he was dead or alive. I called his family, but he had not gone back to Memphis. I called the hospitals to see if he'd been in some sort of accident. I couldn't find him anywhere.

Then, one day he showed up. I later learned that he had gone on a drinking binge and checked into a hotel somewhere until he was able to get over it. But I didn't find that out until much later.

That was the first time I realized something was very wrong with Graves, but it was too late. I was married to him and I was pregnant. One day, he finally confessed, "There's something I haven't told you. You see, I had a nervous breakdown."

I said, "You did? Well that's not so terrible. You can get over a nervous breakdown."

"I know," he said. "But I haven't gotten over it quite yet." What he was trying to tell me was that he was an alcoholic, but I had never seen an alcoholic and did not know anything about alcoholism. My mother did not even know what an alcoholic was. So this news came as a total surprise to everyone.

Alcohol was a challenge to Graves, who felt that his manhood was on the line. After all, everybody else could drink, so why couldn't he? And on top of that, he was violently allergic to it. He would start wheezing and have trouble breathing. It was terrible to watch him, but I didn't know what to do.

The Metropolitan Opera

That same year, besides the stress of coming to terms with Graves' alcoholism, I had my debut at the Met. It was 1951, the same year the celebrated and notorious Rudolf Bing became the director of the Metropolitan Opera Company. Mr. Bing was a very thin man with hawkish features and an outwardly kind manner, which only thinly masked a conniving and manipulative personality. When we first met, he was very nice to me. But before I made my debut, he pulled a knavish stunt.

I was scheduled to record the opera *Die Fledermaus* for RCA Victor. I had worked all summer long with the entire cast and conductor Fritz Reiner. Mr. Reiner was a wonderful conductor of symphony and opera and a great musician himself. We were both scheduled to make our debut at the Met that season and doing the recording was a welcome warm-up for the live performances to come. We were both very excited about it, as well as the prestige the Metropolitan Opera would bring to both our careers. Meanwhile, the album covers for our recording had been printed and we were ready to begin the next day when I got an urgent call to come to Mr. Bing's office. It was just weeks before the season was to begin.

I walked confidently into Mr. Bing's office and sat down for what I assumed would be a discussion about the upcoming performances. I was thrilled to be so close to a dream I'd had since I was 15 years old and just starting to sing. After a moment, Mr. Bing began the conversation.

"Miss Piazza, I understand you are scheduled to record *Fledermaus* for RCA Victor?"

"Yes sir" I said, anticipating his congratulations. "Isn't that wonderful?"

Ignoring my reply, he continued, "Miss Piazza, are you aware that this is an act of disloyalty to the house?"

I was struck dumb. What on earth was he talking about?

Sternly, he clarified, "You know very well that we have signed a contract with Columbia Records to record all the operas."

"Yes, I know," I said. "But what does that have to do with me?"

With a sigh of impatience, he told me that the Met was going to record *Die Fledermaus* and that they might need me. I told him that Ljuba Welitsch, who was also singing *Fledermaus* at the Met, was Columbia's big star. I knew that she would do the part, and the company wouldn't need me. But Bing insisted that I was the one who would back her up if she be unable to perform.

I couldn't believe what I was hearing. It just didn't make sense to me. Surely there would be someone else. Besides, the people recording it with me: Robert Merrill, Patrice Munsel, Jarmila Novotna, were all going to be doing their roles here at the Met, too.

"Why are you singling me out?" I suddenly asked, casting aside my previous politeness. I was beginning to get angry.

Bing answered with an air of reasonableness. "Well, they all have long standing contracts with RCA and I know this is your first project. While I cannot control them, I can do something about you. Miss Piazza, if you make the recording tomorrow, I cannot guarantee your debut at the Met."

Blackmail! I was beside myself with fury, but ultimately, Mr. Bing won. I had to go to Fritz Reiner and tell him I could not do the recording, and why. He cautioned me to hold my ground. "Don't pay him any mind. He's just trying to scare you and control you."

I said, "I know. But he said I wouldn't make my debut and it has already been announced. I have to make the debut. Otherwise, people will say I wasn't good enough."

Reiner thought I was making a mistake and that I should ignore this threat. But I couldn't. "I'm sorry, Mr. Reiner. There's nothing I can do except tell you that I won't be able to do the recording."

Ultimately, they hired soprano Regina Resnick to take my place.

Mr. Bing meant what he said. I went on to make my debut at the Met that season, but Fritz Reiner did not. He moved to Chicago, where he had a long and wonderful career as conductor of the Chicago Symphony. In Mr. Bing's memoir, *5000 Nights at the Opera*, he talks about throwing Reiner out, but he did not mention the incident with me. I know that if I had made that recording, I would not have made my debut at the Met.

To my everlasting regret, it did cost me RCA Victor and all the operatic recordings I would have done. However, life sometimes requires that we make difficult choices. Rudolf Bing presented me with one of my most difficult.

In the fall of 1951, I made my Metropolitan Opera debut in the leading role of Rosalinda in *Die Fledermaus*. My beautiful mother, who looked more like my older sister, arrived from New Orleans a few days before with my son Gregory, who was two years old. Also from New Orleans came my Aunt Ann and my Uncle George with his wife Bobbie, and my friend, Muriel Frances. As usual with my big Italian family and me, chaos reigned. That afternoon, Gregory got sick with a high fever. All of us were worried about him, but I had to go on to the Met, so my mother hired a registered nurse to stay with him.

Backstage, my dressing room was filled with friends and relatives wishing me well before the performance. I purchased a box seat for my mother, Graves, the noted columnist, Earl Wilson and his wife Rosemary, and one other very special guest, Fritzi Scheff.

Fritzi was an elderly lady. She had sung the soubrette part of Adele at the Met the very first time they staged *Die Fledermaus* in 1905. We became friends during a performance of the operetta, *Mademoiselle Modiste*, on NBC, when I sang the part that had been written especially for her by Victor Herbert years before.

We did the entire operetta on TV, writing in a small part for Fritzi so she could be in the little hat shop and sing one chorus of the song "Kiss Me Again", which she had made famous. Fritzi died in 1954, but remains an icon in American musical theatre history.

Now, theatre chimes rang out signaling the audience to take their seats. My mother kissed me and, like the pied piper, led the happy, boisterous group out of my dressing room. Only my publicist, Edgar Vincent, stayed with me while I applied my stage makeup. He was a good-looking young man with dark hair and a sincere interest in his clients.

In the old Metropolitan Opera House, I had a tremendous dressing room with a long vanity top below a long stretch of mirror with lights. Edgar left me alone just as the orchestra started playing the overture. It takes a few minutes before Rosalinda makes her entrance, so I sat there thinking about what I was going to do, and I started to get a little nervous. So I said to myself, "Let me do something to take my mind off this." Looking over at my vanity, I noticed the big pile of tissues I'd used while putting on my makeup.

"I should get rid of that mess," I thought. So I picked it all up and dumped it in the toilet. There was so much of it that it came all the way up to the top. It was an old fashioned toilet with the tank above and a pull string flush. I just knew all that tissue was never going to go down. Then, I got the bright idea to burn it. That way it wouldn't be a mess and I won't stop up the toilet. So I got some matches and threw them on the Kleenex. Being full of the baby oil I use to remove makeup, it started to burn immediately.

What I didn't realize was that the toilet was so old the seat was made of wood and covered in celluloid. Boom! It burst into a gigantic flame. A rush of adrenaline blasted my senses as I thought, "Oh, God, I'm gonna burn down the Met."

I rushed to turn on the faucet in the sink and in full costume, with my hands cupped, was trying to douse the fire when a knock came at the door followed by, "Miss Piazza, you're on!" It was Edgar Vincent. I opened the door and said, "Edgar, I have a fire!"

"Oh, my God!" he cried. Rushing in, he ripped his handkerchief out of his pocket, ran water over it and was trying to put out the huge flame with that tiny handkerchief. Then he looked at me and shouted, "Go. You have to go on." I left him with the fire and walked out on stage to make my debut with one of the grandest of all grand opera companies in the world, not knowing if I would be able to finish it or if the building would have to be evacuated!

The next day, Earl Wilson wrote in his column, "The audience wasn't the only thing Marguerite Piazza set on fire last night!"

Die Fledermaus, by the way, is one of the most difficult operas to sing. The big aria (The Czardas) alone is enough to do you in. I had to put out of my mind my nerves, worries about my unwell son, and the fire burning in my dressing room so I could focus completely on the music, my voice and what was required of me in that moment.

My ability to do just that has been both a challenge and a relief throughout my life. I often pushed myself so hard I made myself sick. But in times of great emotional stress, it was actually a relief to be forced to drop all worry, fear and doubt so I could walk out onto a stage and perform. A performance is a gift. It's an energy exchange with my audience and the payback is huge. Sex gets a lot of attention these days and I'll be the first to admit that great sex can be very gratifying. But it can't hold a candle to the feeling a performer gets from a wildly enthusiastic crowd reaction to a great performance.

A few days before my debut, I was visited by a gentleman who told me he was the head of the "claque." "Miss Piazza," he asked, "how big a claque do you want?"

I said, "A what?" I had never heard of the claque. I was soon informed by other sources that this was an organized group of people who are paid to applaud your performance. They have a union and if you do not hire them, they will boo you. So I asked this man how much they charged and what size I should have. He told me and I hired them on the spot.

Actually, the claque is a very essential part of the opera. A lot of people don't know when and where to clap, and there is definitely an etiquette to follow. The claque takes the worry out of this by leading the audience in applause.

The head of the claque is usually in a prominent location, like a box. He has a handkerchief and when he puts it up, the group applauds. When he puts it down, they are quiet. People enjoy themselves more when there's an enthusiastic audience. If everybody's sitting around on their hands, nobody has a good time. Most artists perform better to an enthusiastic crowd. I even had a friend, Anna Maria Alberghetti, who brought a claque with her to Las Vegas.

But for me, my Aunt Ann was my claque. She laughed at all my jokes and was the first to stand up for an ovation. And she did that without being paid!

I covered several other roles at the Met, but I never had to go in at the last minute for anyone. However, I had to be always prepared. The Met is a repertory company and they have 2nd, 3rd and even 4th covers (substitutes). You were like a doctor on call, and there must always be someone who can fill in for you.

Of all the roles I did learn, *Die Fledermaus* was the only one I sang at the Metropolitan Opera House in New York. It was at the New York City Opera Company where I sang all the parts. I also made guest appearances around the continent with local opera companies such as Toronto, Montreal, St. Louis, New Orleans, Houston and others.

The old Metropolitan Opera House was a fabulously ornate and gilded theater. It was as grand as anything you could find in Europe. After the Met moved to its current location, the old building sat unused for a time. When I learned it was up for sale, in 1966, I tried everything I could to save it from the wrecking ball and almost succeeded. I convinced my friend from Memphis, Kemmons Wilson, the founder of Holiday Inn, to buy it. There were enormous doors that opened onto a huge loading dock that would accommodate very large scenery, which I thought would be the perfect place for the annual New York Auto Show and other events like it.

The price for the building was $3 million, until the owners learned that Kemmons Wilson was interested. Suddenly, it was $9 million. He balked at that and it was torn down to make way for a new office building. I still mourn the loss of such an exquisite piece of architecture.

While I was still on *Your Show of Shows* on NBC, I was scheduled to go on tour with the Met to do 20 more performances of *Die Fledermaus*. I was seven months pregnant and I sang 18 of the 20 performances.

One of the stops along the way was Baltimore, where the theater had a real live resident bat that lived in the auditorium. They tried everything to get rid of him, but couldn't. I was told that he sometimes came down to the stage and flew around. To my dismay, he chose the second act of *Fledermaus* to do just that. He caused such an uproar in the audience that he almost ruined the opera. I was really frightened of him. All I could imagine was this bat getting stuck in my hair. But since "Die Fledermaus" means "the bat" in German, the press had a field day with it.

The day before what would be my last performance with the Metropolitan Opera, I flew to New Orleans to see the doctor who was going to deliver my baby. He was new to me, as I had been seeing a doctor in New York during most of the pregnancy. Jimmy was due in six weeks and I was still happily singing and traveling. The doctors drew blood and ran a battery of tests while I went back to the tour.

I was in a theater in Minneapolis when we got an urgent telephone call from the doctor in New Orleans. He said, "You are so terribly anemic, I don't know what you're operating on. You have got to come back here right now and have a couple of blood transfusions, or I'm not going to be responsible for you."

My husband, Graves, was with me and he put his foot down. "That's it. You're going right to New Orleans and you're not going to finish this tour", he said. I resisted, knowing that the last two performances were in Chicago and they were sold out. But Graves was determined and he wrote a note to Mr. Bing.

During the first intermission, Mr. Bing came backstage and into my dressing room with a great big smile and said, "You were absolutely magnificent! And I want to tell you no one in the audience even noticed you were pregnant. You don't look pregnant at all."

So many of the other prima donnas at that time were big women. I was uncharacteristically petite for an opera singer and all I had to do was put a little bigger skirt around me and it really did not show. When Mr. Bing left, I turned to look at Graves and said, "I guess he hasn't gotten the note yet."

During the second intermission, Mr. Bing came back again. He had received the note by this time, and now he really let me have it. He said, "Let me tell you something. You are going to get on that train tonight and go to Chicago. You will sing those two performances tomorrow!"

But then, Graves cut in and said "Mr. Bing, I don't think you understood what I said. My wife is going to New Orleans tomorrow to have blood transfusions and take care of herself before this baby is born." And that was the end of my career with the Met.

Leaving because of that baby finished it for Mr. Bing and me. He was furious, but I wanted a healthy baby more than I wanted to go on working for him. A few years later, the Met brought a major production to Memphis, Tennessee. When they first started the Guarantors of the Met, my third husband, Billy, and I were among the first Guarantors in my adopted hometown of Memphis.

There was a big reception at the Claridge Hotel. I happened to be momentarily standing by myself, all decked out in evening attire, when the doors opened and two men walked in. To my shock and surprise, they were Mr. Bing and his second in command at the Met, Max Rudolf. They saw a young, pretty matron from Memphis standing there, and Mr. Bing said, "How lovely you look this evening." He took my hand, kissed it, clicked his heels and said, "I'm Rudolph Bing."

I just smiled and said "I'm Marguerite Piazza." He looked up, horrified, dropped my hand and said, "What are you doing here?"

I said, "I'm one of your sponsors."

"Oh," he replied weakly.

Max Rudolf, on the other hand, threw his arms around me, kissed me and said, "Marguerite, I'm so glad to see you." He was still my friend and that felt really wonderful. But even better, I would not have taken a million dollars for the look on Rudolf Bing's face when he realized who I was.

The power plays and the egos at that level are tremendous. One afternoon in the 1980's, I was flipping through a Women's Wear Daily and I saw a picture of Mrs. Bing all dolled up for some function in New York. Her quote, when asked about her husband was this: "Not only does he not listen to opera, he has no social dealings with singers.

But then, he never did." She continued, "Singers? Oh God, no. I never socialized with them. I don't think that in thirty years a singer has entered my apartment.'"

I had to laugh when I read that. If it hadn't been for the blood and sweat of the singers, she wouldn't have her jewels or dress or apartment in New York City. After all, Rudolf Bing got his start as a sales clerk in a music store in Germany. If you want to play the game, it helps to remain grounded and take all that posturing with a grain of salt. Even those at the top of their game are still just human beings like everybody else.

I find it very interesting that even to this day, I am still known as a star of opera. I spent 18 years in supper clubs, but no one thinks of me as a supper club performer. I am the operatic star, "La Piazza." I am from opera. And that is because of TV and NBC's *Your Show of Shows*, not because of the Met. The producer, Max Liebman, gave me the title: "Miss Opera," and no matter what else I did or sang, Marguerite Piazza and opera were forever indelibly linked.

The End of Graves

I took six weeks off just before the baby was born and we went to New Orleans. It was Graves who insisted that I begin to take better care of myself and our unborn child. I have to give him credit for that.

Back in New Orleans, I had an apartment at the Pontchartrain Hotel on St. Charles Avenue. It was such a relief to have the support of my family around me again, but soon after we arrived, Graves disappeared again. I remember looking out the window, down at the street, wondering what had happened to him. He was driving an automobile this time and I prayed that he wouldn't wreck himself or someone else. Eventually, he turned up, always apologetic and usually with an expensive piece of jewelry that was supposed to make up for his absence.

Finally, the baby was born. To Graves' surprise and delight, Jimmy looked just like him! What a change came over the man. All of the sudden, there had never been a baby born in the world except his. His baby was the best, the finest, the greatest thing on Earth. He just worshipped this child, because it was his. But that did not stop Graves' drinking, or the Hell I went through watching him destroy himself.

We went back to New York almost immediately after Jimmy's birth, and I went back to work on *Your Show of Shows*. Life soon became predictable. Graves usually picked Friday night to get drunk—an event that was just torture for both of us. I was up all night working with him, trying to sober him up or at least get him to go to sleep.

He would want to leave the apartment, but I could see that he could hardly walk. How could he leave? I also tried to keep him inside because I did not want anyone to know or to see him in that condition. I cannot tell you how many bottles of Scotch I threw down the kitchen sink. I must have poured them out by the case--good, expensive, 12-year-old Scotch. I didn't care. I just wanted it out of his reach, and out of our house.

When things got really bad, Graves would call the doctors to come and take care of him, or he would call an ambulance to take him to the hospital. In those days, alcoholism was not treated like a disease, as it is today. Not knowing any better, I felt that he didn't need a hospital. He was just terribly drunk.

All night long, I fought this state he was in and tried everything I knew to make him go to bed. But as drunk as he got, he never forgot phone numbers. He would start telephoning everyone he knew in the middle of the night; whether long distance or around the corner. It was just a horrendous situation.

I still remember taking the phone into the closet and calling my mother in New Orleans. I'd say, "I cannot stand it another minute. Please come up here." She would drop everything she was doing and come to New York. But the minute my mother got there, Graves would leave and drive to Memphis. If the police stopped him in the car, he would pay them to drive him the rest of the way to wherever he was going. And in those days, they would do it.

Graves regularly ran off to hotels for several days without any word of where he was or how he was. Then he would come back and be fine for a week or two, sometimes a month. But then, just when I thought things were getting better, he would go off the deep end again.

Finally, one evening, I said to him, "I cannot stand this anymore" and I pleaded with him to let me go. "Let me be free."

But no, he would not. Once when he was really, really drunk, he took me by the throat and said, "I could kill you." And I said, "Go ahead. It's not worth living this kind of a life. I would just as soon be dead." And I meant it.

Instead, he let me go and started to cry. He said, "You know it's not me. It's the liquor talking."

But I was used to this argument. "I don't care. I just want to be free of you and free of it. Please let me go," I pleaded.

All this time I had to be at the NBC studio at 8:30 a.m. to begin rehearsal. And I could not say a word to anybody about what was going on. In fact, I thought no one knew. I kept it totally to myself thinking, if NBC knew I was married to an alcoholic! My God, that would be awful. Besides worrying about what other people would think, the stress of the situation was physically debilitating. It got more and more difficult to keep up my façade of a happy marriage while also maintaining a demanding singing career.

When I had about all I could take and there was nowhere else to turn, I went to St. Patrick's Cathedral and I prayed. I knew there was no way for me to live in that confused and chaotic state any longer. So I offered God my life. I literally prayed, "God, please do something. Either take me or take him because I can no longer live like this." In two weeks, Graves McDonald was dead.

Graves had a European doctor in New York. He called him one time when he was drunk and the man came to our apartment and gave him a shot. Graves went right to sleep. Then this doctor came into the living room and sat down. He said to me, "He's a very strong man."

I agreed.

He continued, "By now, he should be addicted."

I said, "What do you mean?"

The doctor confided. "I've been giving him morphine."

I couldn't believe it! This doctor went on to tell me that he'd been giving Graves morphine to get him addicted to it instead of alcohol. He said he had lots of people who came to his office every day to get their shot of morphine.

I was in shock.

He added, "Wouldn't you rather have him just come to my office every day for a shot of morphine than to drink and be ranting and raving all the time?"

I said, "No! You have no right to do that to this man. You know what you are? You are a devil. Get out of my house. And don't you ever come back here again." I should have called the American Medical Association, but I didn't know about that organization at the time.

It wasn't long afterwards that Graves died. He had been in a hotel somewhere, drunk, and he called this same doctor who came over and gave him a shot of morphine on top of all that alcohol. After the doctor left, he fell down in the bathroom and passed out, landing on his back. When he regurgitated, he choked on his own effluvium and died.

The second person to call and tell me Graves was dead was the doctor. Hal Janis, the assistant producer of *Your Show of Shows*, was the first. Hal came over to get me and took me to Graves by way of back doors and service elevators so I wouldn't have to deal with the press. But the press found out almost before I did. Then, it was front-page news, headlines with pictures. Hal Janis and NBC protected me and I will always be grateful for that.

Sometime after I returned from the funeral in Memphis, I offered Graves' clothes to Hal. They were wonderful, expensive clothes and the men were about the same size. But Hal flatly refused them by saying, "Thank you, Marguerite, but I could never wear anything that belonged to that man after the way he treated you." And I had thought no one knew!

I hardly slept at all the night Graves died. And when I did I had the most awful nightmares. I dreamt I saw Graves walking down the hall and into my bedroom, engulfed in flames. Then I woke up, filled with horror.

The next day, I was to take the body back to Memphis on the train. My dear friend, Anna McKenna, went with me and stayed by my side through the whole ordeal. There was also a priest, Father Charles Chapman, the Regent of the Music School at Loyola when I had been there. He always seemed to turn up whenever something important or tragic was happening to me. When I made my debut as Rose Marie at the Chicago Opera House, here came Father Chapman. When I made my debut at the City Center, he showed up. And for my debut at the Met, he was there to cheer me on.

By coincidence, he was in New York for a meeting that day. He called me as soon as he heard the news about Graves and rode the train halfway to Memphis with me to that funeral. Then he got off and went back to New York for the rest of his meetings. He was such a kind man, and I was very grateful he was there for me when Graves died.

The funeral was one of the most dreadful things I have ever gone through. It was at the First Baptist Church in Memphis and a kind clergyman gave the sermon. But, somehow, it was just more than I could take. Graves' mother, who was a real, dyed-in-the-wool Baptist, had thought I was horrible because I was Catholic. I knew Graves had never been baptized, so one day when he was sitting in the living room of our apartment in New York, I went over to him with some water and baptized him. He said, "What are you doing?" So I told him I was baptizing him.

I told his mother that I had been able to do this one day before he died. I don't think she liked that too much, either. I sure hope we have come a long way since then.

My entire association with Graves McDonald lasted only two years. He told me once that if he died with his will in its present condition, that I would call him a son of a bitch. Well, he did and I did. Evidently, he had made the will under pressure from his mother. He told me he wanted to change it, but he never got around to it.

He left his entire estate to his infant son, Jimmy. I went to court to change that so I could have money to live on and continue my apartment and pay my expenses. But it was a nasty court battle. They did things like publish my grocery bill, which was rather high, and listed all the things I had purchased for the apartment in New York.

My mother-in-law thought it was just awful that I challenged the will. But I had to. And finally, I won the case. Since everything was in my hands at that point, so was her house, which Graves owned. Percy McDonald, Sr. came to me one day and informed me of this. He said, "Now, Marguerite, you don't want her house. Why don't you just sign these papers and give her a present of her house."

So I did. I signed the papers and gave her the house, no questions asked. There was no law that said I had to do that; I did it out of the

71

kindness of my heart. I could never put anyone out of their house. But that only made her dislike me more, because now, she was beholden to me.

When Jimmy had his second birthday, she sent him a little suit. It was really lovely and I called to thank her. I said, "Oh Jimmy loves his little suit…" I put it on pretty thick because I wanted to flatter her and make her feel good. I told her I put it on him so he could see himself in it. It was so cute and he just turned around and looked at himself in the mirror. He just loved the little suit his grandmother sent him. Her answer was: "I suppose so. As the mother jackass prances, so will the little one prance behind."

I said, "What did you say, Mrs. McDonald?" And she repeated the whole thing.

I said, "I thought that's what you said. Goodbye, Mrs. McDonald!" And that was the last time I ever spoke with her.

Mrs. McDonald was very hard on Graves when he was a little boy. Her children were all grown when he was born and she was very strict with him. Graves told me he wanted to play baseball on Sunday afternoons, but she wouldn't allow it. Her religion would not allow anything that was entertainment on Sundays.

He was also often denied access to children his own age. I think that caused him great problems later in life. For example, because he was allergic to alcohol, when he was told he couldn't have it, those orders and denial of something he wanted echoed his mother. When he became a grown man, he was going to do it anyway. I believe to this day that the angst going back to his childhood was the root of his problem that made him so sick.

Another problem caused by the will had an adverse affect on my son, Jimmy. Graves left in his will that Jimmy had to go to a public school. He could not go to a religious school and therefore could not go to the Catholic school with the rest of my children.

Actually, the lawyer (as well as the bank holding his trust) told me to go ahead and send Jimmy to the Catholic school with his sisters and brothers, and that no one would object. "We don't object and I'm sure Graves would not object," they said.

Well, guess who objected? Graves' brother, John, went to the bank and made a fuss. Had little Jimmy needed a glass of water to survive, John would not have been there to give it to him. But he took himself to the bank and said, "If you do not see that my nephew goes to a public school, I will attack the judgment and have it broken. And I will claim the money."

I had no other choice but to take Jimmy out of the Catholic school. Fortunately, there was a good public school in our neighborhood and I sent him there.

Husband #3: Billy Condon

I was only a widow for six months when I came back to Memphis and met Billy Condon. I was the only person under contract to NBC at the time with any connections in Tennessee. They needed me there because Ed Sullivan had come to town and there was only one TV station in Memphis then. It was an NBC affiliate and CBS wanted to take it over.

CBS sent Ed Sullivan down to the Cotton Carnival for two weeks, along with a battery of publicity people. Ed appeared at every event and was just about to win that station over to CBS when NBC asked if I would go down and see what I could do.

Although NBC sent only one publicity man with me, I had connections, having been married to Graves. Percy and Jody McDonald picked a young man named Billy Condon to be my escort, and for one solid week, he squired me to everything almost 24 hours a day.

One of the things we did was to go to the Landing of the Barge. It's a huge event and everybody in Memphis shows up on the grand Mississippi riverfront to watch as several magnificently outfitted barges and riverboats make their way toward the downtown skyline. The last barge is an enormous throne carrying the king and queen of the Cotton Carnival through elaborate fireworks that would have put ancient Memphis, Egypt to shame.

When the barge landed, I was there to sing the Star Spangled Banner. It was bitterly cold that night and I wore an evening dress with bare shoulders and a white mink wrap. And because it was freezing, I was also wearing Billy Condon's raincoat.

Fortunately, the effort was well worth it. I saved the station for NBC and it's still the NBC affiliate in Memphis, WMC-TV Channel 5, one of the longest-running stations in the country.

After the Cotton Carnival, I went back to New York and *Your Show of Shows*. Billy came to New York to see me a few times, and after knowing each other for only a few weeks, we decided to get married.

Early one morning in July of 1953, we drove out of Memphis in Billy's new Buick convertible. I remember it well. It was a creamy yellow with red leather upholstery. Here we were with the top down and me with the scarf flowing and the dark glasses. We were going to be married in Mississippi at a little place where no one would know about it.

Ha! That was what we thought. Every little township in Mississippi had a reporter and a photographer at their courthouse. We would drive up, see the reporters sitting on the steps, then take off for the next town.

Finally frustrated, Billy called a friend in Jackson, Mississippi who owned the newspaper there. The friend said to come on down, he would arrange everything. He made a reservation at the hotel in his own name to keep everything quiet. Then he and his wife got the Justice of the Peace and stood for us at the ceremony. Afterwards, we all had dinner together, and the Judge reassured me that I was "just as married as if I had ten bridesmaids."

We stayed at the Heidelberg Hotel that night and the next morning at 7 a.m., there was a knock on the door, followed by, "We know you're in there." A whole battery of photographers was outside our room. Billy answered the door and the first and only time I have ever seen this outside of the movies, that newspaper reporter stuck his foot in the door!

Billy said, "Now, wait a minute, you're not coming in here right now."

But the reporters said, "We know she's in there. We want a picture and we want a story."

Billy wisely agreed, saying, "If you'll let us get dressed, we'll give you both." Delighted, they let us close our door, and we got up, dressed and let them in.

Then we called my mother and went to New Orleans to see her. My poor, dear mother had no idea what was going on. When we arrived, the house was besieged by reporters and photographers and Ma just looked at me and said, "I don't believe you've done this. I just don't believe you've done this again."

Well, I had, and with all those people and all that bedlam, she was having a fit. By the time New Orleans settled down, we returned to Memphis, where Billy and I spent the night at his brother, Martin's, house, only to face another onslaught of reporters and photographers there.

We really got the coverage on that one! But I didn't really mind--I was on top of the world. This time I had found a man that I truly was madly in love with. He was handsome, warm, and funny, and he loved me too. I had everything... a successful career, a loving relationship, and I would soon have a house where I could live with my husband and children, like a real family.

Billy and I lived our first married days together in rooms at the Memphis Country Club, until we rented a house on Rose Road. At that time, I was flying back and forth to New York to do *Your Show of Shows* every week and I couldn't spend a whole lot of time in Memphis. I flew home on Saturday night after the show and stayed through Monday. I had to be back in New York on Tuesday to begin working on the next show. So, of course, I kept the apartment in New York.

We spent that summer looking for a house and finally bought one at 3936 Walnut Grove Road. In between shows, I shopped and fixed and decorated. I guess we were a very early version of the "commuting couple."

I already had Gregory and Jimmy and shortly thereafter, I gave birth to Shirley.

The house was a lovely Georgian style, but not very large, so I built a big playroom onto the side for the children. It had a broken tile floor, which I later regretted. Once when Shirley was still a baby, I had her resting on a pillow on the sofa in that room. One of Billy's cousins, Steve, was there with his kids and they were playing with the baby. One of them accidentally pulled the pillow out from under her and Shirley fell head first onto that hard floor. Luckily, the pillow fell under her and broke the fall.

I was reminded of this recently when one of my grandchildren fell off of a chair. Strangely enough, it was Shirley who grabbed him just in time.

Giving Birth Through Chaos

Billy and I had some traumatic experiences together in that house, especially just before Shirley was born. My husband had one rather serious problem then. He had very bad hemorrhoids that used to bleed all the time. And true to his sense of humor, he used to say it was from reading too many comic books on the john when he was little.

I actually believed him, but one day we decided he should go to a doctor who specialized in such things. He was also a friend and a general surgeon.

He operated on Billy and sent him home a bit too soon. The doctor said everything looked good and we brought him home. I was very pregnant at the time, and I also had a terrible cold. I didn't want to give Billy my cold on top of all the pain he already had, so I slept on the sofa in the little porch-like room off our bedroom suite. That way, I could hear Billy, but would not infect him.

Fortunately, my mother was visiting. She was staying in the other side of the house with Gregory and Jimmy. I heard Billy stirring, but I was sleepy and didn't get up. I called out "Are you all right?" He kept saying yes.

When he was hurting, the doctor told him to sit in a hot tub of water, which he did for a while. Then he got back in bed. When he finally called for help, I found him in a pool of blood that must have been 24 inches across.

I immediately called the doctor and told him what condition Billy was in. He said he was sending an ambulance right away and that he would meet us at Baptist Hospital. I told Billy to hold on, then woke up my mother to tell her I was going to the hospital with Billy. The ride was on a road that was, in those days, very bumpy and I know every pothole was painful for him.

For some reason, Billy had the good sense to hang his head over the side of the gurney to keep the blood going to his brain. As soon as we got to the hospital doors, they were waiting for us with more blood. They put it into his arm before he even got out of the ambulance, then took him right to the operating table.

I went to his hospital room to wait while they sewed up that vein that was gushing so badly. Besides being life-threatening to Billy, this whole experience was very traumatic for me and I started to dilate. When he finally came out of the operating room and I saw he was going to be all right, I told him I had to go home and get some rest myself.

Although I was not supposed to give birth for another six or seven weeks, I was so exhausted that when I went home, my mother put me on the pullout sofa so I wouldn't have to climb the stairs.

Chaos continued to arrive at our house. The next event was centered around two-year-old Jimmy, who had a lollypop in his mouth. When he finished it, he kept the stick in his mouth. I kept asking him to take it out, but he wouldn't listen to me. I was too weak to get up and take it away from him, but suddenly, he fell down and this stick, which had a point on it, was pushed into the roof of his mouth.

Of course, he screamed. My adrenaline started to flow and I jumped up from my sofa bed, pulled that thing out of his mouth, picked him up and felt my water break.

Now they had to rush me, with my son, Jimmy, to the hospital. It was literally one crisis after another. Billy was recuperating in one hospital and here I was in another one trying not to have a baby. Finally, the doctor said, "This is foolish. That baby is coming whether we like it or not." And she did. We named her Shirley, after my mother-in-law.

There was a lot of history behind that name. We had a running skit on *Your Show of Shows* where Sid Caesar and Imogene Coca played two crazy factory workers. I don't remember what his name was, but her name was Shirley, and they called her "Shoil." Because of that skit, I thought Shirley was the worst name in the world.

However, it was my mother-in-law's name and she had six granddaughters, none of whom had been named Shirley. I figured I had to do it. So, biting the bullet, I named my beautiful child a name I detested.

My sister-in-law said, "Mother doesn't care about that. You didn't have to name her Shirley." But when my mother-in-law came to the hospital to see the new little Shirley, she said to the nurse, "What's her second name?" The nurse said the second name was Marguerite. "Oh" she said disapprovingly. She wanted Shirley to have both her names!

As it turned out, my daughter, Shirley, has made it a beautiful name and one to be loved, because Shirley is all about love.

Life Magazine Comes to My Party

Once we were in the house on Walnut Grove Road, we had a lot of good times. I remember that one day, we decided to have a big, beautiful party. I wanted it to be an Italian "festa," and I researched for two months to find out all the things they did at the country festas in Italy. I learned about stomping on the grapes to make wine, dancing the Tarantella, and climbing a greased flagpole. And yes, we did it all.

The greased flagpole was great fun, and the object was to make it to the top. I had thought I would just have the flagpole installed in my yard, grease it up and that no one would actually attempt to climb it. I guess I didn't really know my guests, because three people actually made it to the top! They were so proud of themselves--until they saw the prize for getting there was a real, live goat!

Some serious planning and organization went into this party. We had a small party every night for a week to prepare and to learn the Tarantella. Life Magazine sent two photographers to do a piece called, "Life Goes to a Party."

I had the reporters in my house as guests for a week. We wined and dined them, took them to the Hunt and Polo Club, did everything for these two photographers. I had a dance master from Italy who came every night to give lessons to Billy and me and 6 of our friends who volunteered to learn and perform the Tarantella.

I flew in the canoli from New Orleans, and I had pasta with meatballs and Sicilian sausage and just about anything you can think of. And, of course, we had a huge trough made and filled it with a truckload of grapes. You've never seen so many grapes in all your life.

My dear friend, Dudley Fulton (a beautiful woman with long red hair and a fantastic artist) and I got in the trough and stomped the grapes with our bare feet. The juice ran out into a vat and we had a fabulous time.

I brought in a band called "Jimmy Mahanna's," and had them all dress up in gondolier's hats and sashes, which I supplied. They also learned to play some Italian folk songs.

Everything was decorated like an Italian festa. I found some people who made a big arch for me that lit up and said "Beinvenuto" in little white lights. At four in the afternoon, it clouded up and we thought it was going to storm and ruin everything. So I promised St. Theresa a lot of money if she would just hold the rain until after the party was over. And she did, so I paid it.

As you might expect, after all this effort, the two reporters from Life Magazine were unable to get a single picture out of it. Something happened to the film, they said, and the article never appeared. It didn't matter, as it was the source of wonderful memories for everyone who attended.

The House That Became My Home

No sooner had we gotten fixed, furnished, carpeted and really settled in, when I saw it—the house of my dreams. I had gone to look at houses with my friend, Jody McDonald, when we saw the most wonderful old house on Central Avenue. It was enormous. There were three stories plus a basement and a carriage house. It had been completed about 1910, and while it needed quite a bit of work, it was really a grand old house.

Jody said that it was just too big for her, but I was crazy about it. When I got home that afternoon, I told everyone I had been looking for houses with Jody, but I didn't mention the house on Central. That was on Friday, and my mother was visiting.

On Monday, she was leaving for New Orleans and Billy drove her to the train station because she hated airplanes and refused to fly. When they were driving down Central Avenue, she saw the Immaculate Conception Church and School. Then she looked across the street and saw this big house for sale.

She said, "Oh, Billy, look at that house for sale. And it's across the street from the church and school. Why don't you drive around the block so we can see it again." He said, "M, you're gonna miss your train."

"No, we're not. Go around the block once." They drove around the block and looked at it again. My mother said, "That is a great house. Promise me you'll go and see it." He promised. Then he put her on the train, went back to his office, called the real estate people and went to see the house. At noon, he called home and said, "Marguerite, I want you to come and look at this house. It's beautiful and I really like it."

I asked him where it was and he said, "Central and Belvedere." I said, "Across from the church and school? I've seen it." He said,

"Well, what did you think?" And I said, "If I hadn't just bought a house and fixed it all up, I would have bought this one. I loved it." Then he asked me if I wanted it and I said yes. At three o'clock that same day, we owned it. We walked down the stone steps in the front yard as another couple was walking up. Billy just smiled at them and said, "You're too late. We just bought it." And that was the beginning of our house on Central Avenue. That night when we got home we suddenly realized, Oh, no! We have two houses. We have to get rid of one of them.

We stayed in the old house for about six more months while I replaced all the wiring and updated the plumbing in the new house. But even after we moved in, I continued to build, remodel, decorate and fix it for over thirty years.

Commuting Takes Its Toll

When my daughter, Shirley, was born in the early spring of 1954, I was still commuting to New York for *Your Show of Shows.* I remember trying to get back in time for her christening on Sunday morning. I did the show Saturday night, and Hal Janis had arranged for me to sing for the police department in Connecticut right after the show was over. He drove me, I sang and then he drove me back to the airport in New York just in time to catch the midnight flight home.

I arrived in Memphis about 5 am, but by the time I got home it was almost seven. The christening was at ten, and of course we were having a party after it was over. The children's nurse, Rebecca, who was absolutely indispensable, had everything planned and ready to go. So I went straight into my dressing room to change. Billy and I had been to Paris, where I bought some wonderful perfume; big bottles of the stuff. They were all in the bottom drawer of my dressing table.

I picked one up and found to my surprise that it was empty. I picked up another one and it was empty, too. They were all empty. I went screaming out of the room to Rebecca, "What's happened to all my French perfume? Where is it?" She said, "I was hoping you wouldn't notice it until after the christening. I went to the store to get what we needed for this party and I left Jimmy with one of the maids. She wasn't watching as she should have been and he went into your room, pulled out all the bottles of perfume, uncorked them and poured them all out onto the carpet."

80

I just collapsed onto the floor and cried. They were so expensive and so wonderful, and I was so exhausted. They had washed the rug and left the windows open for days trying to get the smell aired out. Was there any punishment? No, for little Jimmy was only three years old, so what could I do? After all, it was only perfume.

Help Along The Way

When I moved from New York to Memphis to live, I had Gregory, who was five and Jimmy, who was almost two. I had a German nurse who came with me and stayed in Memphis for a while. I was in a difficult situation with my career and my children. I had to have someone to take care of the children, someone I could trust. It is very difficult, if not impossible, to be completely sure of someone you hire to come into your home. But this woman had been with me for a while and I trusted her.

It wasn't until my mother came to visit and overheard her with Jimmy that I realized what was going on. She had taken over Jimmy to a point where she was trying to turn him against me. My mother heard her say to him one day: "Talk up to her. Defend yourself." This is a two-year-old she was talking to. "They don't do anything for you," she said. "I do everything for you. I'm more your mother than she is. Talk back to her and tell her."

When my mother told me this, I fired the nurse and sent her back to New York. Now I had to find another nurse or I couldn't do *Your Show of Shows* or anything else. We hired one lady who didn't work out, so we fired her. Then another one came for an interview. She picked up little Shirley, and Billy took one look at her and grabbed Shirley out of her arms. Billy said, "I'll take Shirley upstairs and put her to bed." The search continued.

The next day, we interviewed another lady--one who would become a powerhouse in my life. Her name was Rebecca Franklin, or Becky, as we came to call her. Becky had nursed the children of a couple of families in Memphis. They were people I knew, and they spoke very highly of her. In fact, there were really only two professional nurse-governesses in the city of Memphis. One was Becky and because she was available, we hired her on the spot.

Becky took over the household immediately. She saw exactly what was needed and she took care of it, becoming like a second mother to the children. In addition to that, she completely ran my house, going to the grocery store and planning and buying everything we needed. We gave her a check once a week to cover all necessities, and in time, we trusted her to hire household staff and tell them what to do. She also paid them and, when necessary, fired them. She even hired a man to take care of the yard. She just did everything. And she was great.

We were disappointed when Becky left us after her marriage to Don Franklin, but were delighted when she came back to us about a year later, during which we had moved into the big house on Central Avenue. Both she and Don moved into an apartment in our house and, at the height of all the kids and all the help, I think I was feeding around 13 people, three meals a day, every day.

Becky had only one 24 hour day off every two weeks; on that day, we had a substitute nurse. Even though Becky and Don had an apartment over the carriage house, she slept in a connecting room off the children's room. If one of those babies was sick in the middle of the night, she was right there. Becky was on call 24 hours a day, even in her sleep!

But Becky did more than take excellent care of my children. I could say, "We're having ten people for dinner tomorrow" (or even tonight) and walk out of the house, and she would handle everything. She planned the meal, she bought it, decorated it, set the table, made sure the house was immaculate and made sure the meal was served properly. She instructed the cook, the maid and the yardman along the way, all the time with my children underfoot!

In my house, we had a staff, as they say in England, and it was wonderful. For eighteen years, that's the way we lived. Becky brought every baby home from the hospital and loved it and took care of each one. She was especially close to little Billy, who was born two months premature, weighing just over five pounds. She brought him home and stayed up with that child for two months. He had the same ailment the Kennedy baby had after being born breech. His lungs had been full of fluid and although they dried up and he was fine, she still watched him, day and night, night and day. She never let him out of her sight.

I could never have lived as I did without Becky. She loved and took care of us all just as if we were her family. And in the end, I guess that's what we were.

Rose Marie in 1946

Marguerite in Vagabond King

Karl Kritz, Hedda Hopper, Marguerite

Desert Song 1947

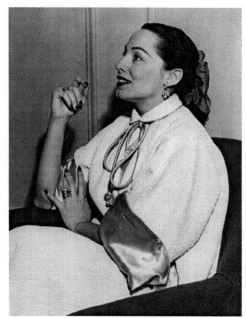

Marguerite Backstage

Marguerite's Aunt Ann Hefter

Happy as Larry with Burgess Meredith

Marguerite and Max Liebman

Your Show of Shows

Singing with Robert Merrill

West Point Cape Fitting with Mr. Fred

Marguerite with Sid Caesar and Wife 1997

Easter Show on NBC 1951

Jimmy

Piazza Parasol 1951

Marguerite and Graves McDonald at the Met

Marguerite in Die Fledermaus

Marguerite, Graves, and son Jimmy 1952

Part Four

The Business of Singing

Up to a certain point in my career, I had never had a professional manager. My husband always took care of the business details. Graves McDonald was very good where finances were concerned and he did me the biggest favor of all. He took my entire salary from *Your Show of Shows* and whatever else I did and bought stock. It was one of the most intelligent things anyone has ever done for me.

After Graves died, I began to look seriously for a manager and soon met Raymond Katz. Raymond was the manager of a radio station in New York City at the time. His mother had a cousin who was married to a movie producer at MGM, so talent management must have seemed like a logical step for Raymond.

I was his first client, but in all the years he was my manager, we never had a written contract. All of our business was done with a handshake. Both Raymond and his mother, Minn, became like family to me and I trusted them implicitly.

Raymond started out by getting me guest jobs on a lot of TV shows like The Jack Parr Show, The Joey Bishop Show, The Ed Sullivan Show and Walter Winchell's "Orchid Award" Show, which was live every Sunday afternoon.

The week I appeared on Walter Winchell's show, Cyd Charisse and Tony Martin opened the show, after which I was to sing a song and receive the Orchid Award. At that time, the CBS studio was on 67th Street, not far from Central Park West. We planned to do the opening number outside, walking down Central Park West with a hookup to the studio. CBS barricaded one whole block and hired a balloon man, an organ grinder with a monkey, and people to pass me as I was walking down the street.

Meanwhile, the orchestra was playing live in the studio and I was singing to that music, which was piped to the street over a loudspeaker. They wanted Cyd Charisse and Tony Martin, who had just finished their segment, to walk past me, nod and wave, while I was singing, "It's a lovely day today for whatever you've got to do..." However, Tony accidentally stepped on the cable connecting the sound of the orchestra to the loud speakers.

Suddenly, I was singing and there was no music. And this was live! So, I just kept singing. I had no idea if I was with the orchestra or not. All you can do in a situation like that is keep going and pray. But it was an ill-fated show from the beginning.

After this fiasco, I ran inside and changed into an evening dress while Walter Winchell was talking. The studio was an old theater with all the ropes hanging down backstage, and I was supposed to walk in and around the ropes as I sang my next song. My dress was strapless and zipped up the side under my arm. However, when the dresser pulled on the zipper, it broke. The timing on a live TV performance is split second and that zipper was not moving. Fortunately, the dresser had one, good-size straight pin on her apron, so she grabbed the two pieces of dress at the top and pinned them together with the straight pin. I had to help keep the dress up by holding it together at the waist with my hand, walking sideways.

Since the dress was strapless, I had absolutely nothing on underneath. A wardrobe malfunction in those days truly would have been a disaster. I prayed awfully hard that dress would stay up. In the end, it did, and I received the Orchid Award. That was one flower I really felt I deserved!

Supper Clubs: "The Act"

I had been on *Your Show of Shows* for four years when it went off the air. That same night, Sid Caesar's new dresser came up to me backstage and said, "Oh, Miss Piazza, do you speak English?"

Shocked, I replied, "What do you mean? I was born in New Orleans, Louisiana. I'm an American!"

"Well," he said, "You always sing in a foreign language and you always wear those big skirts and wigs. I thought you were a foreigner."

This got me thinking. I wondered if a lot of other people in the United States also thought the same thing. If so, I should do something to correct this impression. Then, Raymond came up with the idea that I should do a supper club act, and suddenly, I found myself looking forward to singing popular music, which was what I had done as a kid.

We hired Herbert Ross, who was at that point the choreographer for the Milton Berle Show. He had not yet enjoyed a major success on his own. Together, we three created a very successful enterprise.

Raymond, Herb and I invented what I refer to as "The Act." No one had done anything like it in supper clubs. Before that, everybody in supper clubs, from Sinatra to Helen O'Connell, just stood up in front of a band and sang songs. But I put on a show. It was really almost a review.

I remember calling my mother in New Orleans after it was all set to tell her what I would be doing. I was so afraid she wouldn't approve of my leaving opera to sing in nightclubs. Then, I waited to hear the phone drop. But instead of the phone dropping, she said, "That's great! You should have done it sooner."

The first act, designed and choreographed by Herb Ross, began with the *Comedia del Arte*, the Italian Comedia, and I was dressed in a traditional Columbine outfit with the ruffles around the top, a short, pleated skirt and a little hat with ribbons. The dancer we hired, Jack Bunch, had on a tight outfit with a Harlequin diamond-shaped pattern and a skullcap on his head. The costumes were beautifully designed: classic Comedia.

Jack Bunch was absolutely brilliant. He was a magnificent dancer himself, but he did everything to show me off. He played everything from servant to lover in the form of dance. Jack had the acting ability, the knowledge, the dancing ability, the stable ego and everything else to program it so that I was truly presented, which was what we hired him to do.

The *Comedia del Arte* was entirely in Italian. In my Italian Comedia dress, I sang "La Danza" while Jack danced all around me. Behind me were four poles with a banner stretched across them reading MARGUERITE PIAZZA. As Jack danced, he turned the banners around revealing four *Comedia del Arte* figures. Then, we did several other numbers in Italian. Suddenly, the music stopped and I looked out into the audience and said my first words in English, "Now I'd like to sing Cole Porter."

The pianist, Willie Kaplan, slammed the cover over the piano keys, making a big noise and jolting the audience. Then he said to me on stage, "I'm surprised at you, Miss Piazza. You can't sing Cole Porter in that costume."

I would innocently ask, "Why not?"

"It's wrong," he would say. "All wrong. To sing Cole Porter you have to be slinky, minky, diamond on the pinky."

To which I'd reply, "Indeed? Then I'll change."

"Well, how on Earth are you going to do that?" he'd ask, looking skeptical, to which I'd reply, "In one minute. Gentlemen, set your watches!"

And of course, everyone looked at their watches.

While I was talking to the pianist, Jack would move behind me, take the banners off the pole and drop them on the floor. Then he would bring over the four poles and put them around me at four corners.

As I said, "Gentlemen, set your watches," Jack would hang a special piece of striped green and gold silk around me on the four poles. Now all you could see was my head, my legs and my feet. I woud pull the zipper down and the Comedia dress would fall off me. Then, I would turn it inside out and hand it over the curtain to the dancer, who would hand me a pink satin wraparound skirt.

I already had on a pink satin strapless leotard with a beaded bosom under the first outfit, and the short skirt would go on over that. Then the dancer would bring me another dress, folded inside out so no one could see it. All this time, I would be singing, "Hurry Hurry, Hurry, I'll be dressed in a minute," a special piece written for the show and lasting exactly one minute. The dress that went over the leotard and skirt had long sleeves and wrapped around me with three buttons just under the bust, which was cut out so the beaded top of the leotard looked like part of the dress.

Now, I was ready for the next two parts of the show. The last thing the dancer brought me was a white mink stole and a red satin pillow with a huge fake diamond ring on it. When I got that on, there was a drum roll, the stage went black, and Jack would drop the silk banner around me in the dark. As the lights came on again, I would say, "Slinky, minky, diamond on the pinky," which are the last words to the dressing song.

Then I would tell the piano player, "Now, if you're satisfied, let's kick ole Cole around a little."

And Willie would look at me and go, "Yes, Ma'am!"

That's when I would go over, sit on the piano, and sing 'I've Got You Under My Skin'. After that, I would climb down and sing a few more of Cole Porter's tunes, as well as some other popular songs of the day. And this would bring us to the point where I said, "And now, I'd like to sing you some songs from my home town."

As the orchestra struck up The Muscrat Ramble, I would unbutton the three buttons on my dress, open it up, and reveal a Dixieland Jazz outfit. When I dropped the dress on the floor, the dancer, who had been gone during the pop routine, came back dressed like a bartender with tight black pants and a white shirt with garters and a black bowler hat. He would hand me a pink velvet bowler hat with sequins that matched my outfit. I really loved that old pink derby--I made a lot of money with it and it has a special place in my closet. Every once in a while I get it out, dust it off and take my Dixieland Jazz routine back to the stage.

The Dixieland Jazz routine is an exciting medley of songs that really charges a room with energy. Those songs included, 'Way Down Yonder in New Orleans', 'Dixie', 'Birth of the Blues', and, for a finale, 'When the Saints Go Marching In.'

Five members of the band shed their jackets to reveal red suspenders and garters on their sleeves. They all donned black bowler hats and came out of the orchestra to stand behind me like a marching band. Then, in single file, we marched around the room singing and playing. They really turned the music on full blast, high-stepping and moving all over the place. In New Orleans, this is called "second lining" and it really wakes up an audience.

"The Act" was a sensation in New York. An article in Variety said, "A new form of show business has been born!" Life Magazine did a big article on the show calling me a "Diva in Dixie." Time, Newsweek and all the papers also carried the story.

We opened that show at The Pierre Hotel in New York City in January, 1955, when John Paul Getty owned it. He had a party for me afterwards and I remember someone saying, "Well, you're sure to have a full house and make a lot of money off this show."

Mr. Getty said, "We don't have the Cotillion Room to make money. The reason we have this beautiful room is for publicity for the hotel." Anyway, he sure got publicity for the hotel with my act. I played the

Pierre twice a year for a month at a time, two shows a night, six nights a week. It was rough, but I loved every minute of it.

Richard Nixon

Before we opened the first "Act" in New York, we took it to Washington D.C., totally unannounced, to try it out in front of an audience. The club was rather small and the room really wasn't set up for big shows. They usually just had a trio. But we needed a venue to test the orchestrations, check the costumes, and see if I could do everything in the time allotted.

We got through the first show and I thought no one knew I was in Washington. But for the second show, all the political people started showing up. There was no backstage at all, so I stood just inside the entrance in my *Comedia del Arte* costume and greeted people as they came in.

On the second night, I was very surprised to see the Vice President of the United States come in with his wife. Richard and Pat Nixon said they heard I was breaking in a new show and they were very excited about seeing it. There was a photographer there who asked to take our pictures, so we posed and I thanked them for coming. We became friends after that and later on, when it was very important to me after my radical cancer surgery, the first show I did was to sing the National Anthem for President Nixon at his first Inaugural Gala. I thought Dick and Pat were both wonderful people and he really gave me a new lease on life by asking me to sing when he did. I will always be grateful to him for that.

Jack Paar

Soon after opening that first act in New York, I appeared on the Jack Paar Show. That was a fun show. The renowned Mr. Joseph of Joseph Shoes made me a pair of shoes with clear acrylic heels especially for the show that lit up every time I took a step. All the kids have them today, but in 1955, nobody had ever seen anything like that. I kept them hidden until I walked out on stage, and Jack Parr just had a fit over the "twinkle heel" shoes. It was great fun.

I appeared on Jack's show several times. He was the nicest and most genuine person in the business. Always a great interviewer, he never said anything derogatory. His intention was always to stay positive and to boost you, which today seems to be a lost art. Jack Paar was a wonderfully unique individual.

The Ed Sullivan Debacle

The Ed Sullivan Show was going strong when I opened my first act at the Pierre in New York. Ed came to see me there and afterwards came up to my suite to talk. He spent some time with me and said he wanted to put almost the whole act on his show. I agreed to do it, but by the time I went on, it had been cut to one or two numbers plus the Dixieland Jazz ending. The day of the show I had a touch of the flu and even a fever, but my voice was fine and I decided to go on anyway. I wasn't paying a whole lot of attention to how they were filming me because I really was sick. I was just trying to make it through as best I could.

For the finale, I had on the Dixieland Jazz outfit, which consisted of silk tights and a pink satin leotard heavily lined with stiff cotton to make it tight fitting. It was also structured with whale bones or stays. The outfit was so heavy I could practically stand it up in the corner. On top of that, I had a pink satin wraparound skirt that hooked together at one side of the front of my body. When my leg showed through, it was flattering, but far from obscene. My body was well covered. I may have given the appearance of nakedness, but I was in skin-colored tights and as thoroughly covered as anyone could be.

The show was broadcast live from an old theater. One camera was in the orchestra pit, shooting up at the stage. I noticed it, but really didn't pay any attention to it. There were also two cameras out front and one overhead. Whoever was directing in the booth had all those pictures in front of him, and he decided which camera would be broadcasting at any given moment.

After I did that one show, I never heard from Ed Sullivan again. I didn't know what was wrong. Raymond would call him and say, "Marguerite would like to be on the show again," and he always had an excuse not to have me on. Years later, when he was still on TV, Raymond asked him why he wouldn't have me on his show. Ed Sullivan said, "I don't want anyone on my show that does what she does." When Raymond probed further, Ed Sullivan said, "She moved the slit in her skirt from the side to the middle so that the camera could shoot up her legs and show her crotch!"

Well, I went crazy when I heard that. It never has been my nature to do anything like that. If they got my crotch on camera, they couldn't have seen anything but pink satin. Besides, the man responsible for shooting me from below was the director, who happened to be Ed Sullivan's son-in-law! If Ed Sullivan got any flack about the show from the network or maybe a sponsor, it's possible he wanted to protect his family member and blame me for a bad shot. Regardless, I was furious.

Raymond suggested that I write a letter saying I was sorry this had to happen. I told him I didn't need to write that creep a letter--he should apologize to me! But Raymond insisted that I write him a letter so we'd get back on the show.

I wrote the letter, but it did not please him. Then, I demanded to see the film of that show to learn just how bad it was. Of course, he refused. Finally, I threatened to go to the Archbishop. Sullivan was a Catholic and was very buddy-buddy with the Archbishop at St. Patrick's Cathedral in New York. I wanted to tell the Archbishop just what kind of a guy his friend was, but Raymond wouldn't let me do it. I never did get to see a copy of that show and it is lost from the record. I believe Sullivan destroyed it.

As a manager, Raymond did not always do the best job of protecting me. In a strange way, we had a love-hate relationship. He did things for me, but then he did things that cost me. For instance, Tennessee senator Albert Gore, Sr. invited me to Washington D.C. to sing for the first Congressional Wives Luncheon, given for Jackie Kennedy. I was supposed to stay over and do something for the White House, but Raymond had booked me for a show in New York. He insisted that the show in New York was more important and I assumed he would take care of the politics.

Alas, he did not. I bore the brunt of not doing that second performance in Washington, and years later, the press secretary had still not forgiven me. In fact, when my daughter, Shirley, graduated from Mount Vernon, Liz Carpenter, former press secretary to Lyndon Johnson, was the speaker. I went up to her after the graduation to tell her how much I enjoyed her speech. When I said, "I'm Marguerite Piazza," she reeled away from me as if I were a snake. I couldn't believe how hostile she was toward me after all those years.

Fortunately, our close mutual friend, Maxine Messinger, intervened and explained what happened, and afterward, Liz became my friend.

My Aunt Ann used to get upset that Raymond never said, "You were terrific" to me after a performance. Sometimes I had the feeling he was trying to keep me in the dark about things. Other times he made me feel incapable of doing certain things. I'm not quite sure what motivated that. After all, when I hired Raymond as my manager, he did not get a green, wet-behind-the-ears kid off the street; he got a star. I had already been on *Your Show of Shows* and sung at the Metropolitan Opera.

Despite our constant push and pull, I must say that when I needed his support most, during my radical cancer surgery, Raymond did fly to New York to be with me.

Raymond and his beloved mother, Minn, lived in an apartment on 57th Street. After my mother died, Minn became a sort of surrogate mother to me. I often stayed at their apartment and I never went anywhere without Minn knowing about it. Since I was married and commuting from Memphis, I wasn't dating and I allowed Raymond and Minn to dictate my social life in New York. I was very close to both of them and I thought I was family.

In the beginning, before I met Billy, I think Raymond wanted to marry me, and Minn might even have approved. But then I came home to New York after meeting Billy Condon in Memphis, and my world had changed. Raymond and I went out that night, and when we returned to my apartment, he decided to come upstairs with me. I felt as if he had romantic intentions, so I turned to him on the stairs and said, "Raymond, let's play gin." I knew he liked to play cards.

He said, "You don't know how to play gin."

And I said, "I can try."

He said, "No thanks, Honey." He knew right then and there that if he had been planning anything, it was over.

Taking my Show on the Road: Supper Clubs 1955 - 1969

Las Vegas

I spent a lot of time in Las Vegas. I loved Vegas in those days, except for one thing. Because it was in the middle of a desert, there was very fine sand in the air all the time. This can be a singer's demise. When I arrived in Vegas for the first time, I spent the afternoon rehearsing the band. That night I sang two shows and my vocal chords just couldn't take it. By the second day I was hoarse. It would have been nice to rest for one day, but in Vegas, you worked seven days a week.

Most entertainers working that kind of schedule don't rehearse. They send in their piano player to rehearse the band for them. But not me. I had to be there to hear it for myself. I had to sing and I paid for it.

Those two little vocal chords are actually very tender and delicate and to put them through the workout I gave them was almost more than they could handle. As a result, I was very conservative with my voice during the day. I usually kept completely silent. If I had a phone call, my Aunt Ann took it and, if necessary, she would interpret. At times, it felt as if I were in a monastery. To get the perfection from myself that I demanded, this was how I had to live when working those clubs. I needed extreme rest and quiet time just to be able to summon up all that vivacity and power on stage.

There was a doctor at one of the hotels who was an old alcoholic, but all he would give me was some sort of tonic with alcohol in it. Several times I went to the hospital where they gave me shots of cortisone to clear the vocal chords. In those days, the doctors around the entertainment business didn't care how much they gave you, just as long as the show went on. A lot of entertainers suffered dearly from excessive amounts of cortisone but, thank heavens, I wasn't one of them.

The people in Vegas were great, and really took care of me. My Aunt Ann used to stay backstage in the dressing room with me until after the last show every night, which would sometimes be two or three o'clock in the morning. Ann would busy herself taking care of the props and costumes while I removed the heavy makeup, relaxed for a few minutes and got dressed. Then we would go out into the room, by way of the stage.

In the front of the room at The Sands was a line of booths where you could always find the maître d' (who absolutely controlled the room), Mr. Kelley, with his big cigar and his business associates. It was just as you'd imagine in the movies. They would say hello to us as we passed, which my Aunt Ann recently described to me as "Hey, babe. Where you kids goin'? These are my friends."

We always said a brief hello, then found a table where we could have a late supper. They knew that I was a "good girl," so to speak, and that I didn't fool around with strange men or dope. These people know everything about you when they hire you and they watch you like a hawk when you're there. You can't fool them. And since that's the way I was, they decided they would keep me that way.

Ann and I usually ordered some food, and she would play the slot machines a bit. But if anyone walked over to my table, a giant in a uniform would immediately appear and just stand next to them. If the person didn't behave or said something out of line, this guy would say, "Miss Piazza, you OK?" That was usually enough to move the person along.

My protectors would watch during my act, too. Nobody spoke while I was singing. If someone was making a disturbance, they received one warning to be quiet. If they didn't comply, two big bouncers would come down the aisle, pick them up and very quietly take them outside, no questions asked.

Many of my friends came to Vegas to see me, and after the show we often went out. When we stopped by the front desk to turn in our keys, I would tell the clerk that we were going to whatever hotel it was to catch their late show. By the time we arrived, our table was ready.

Another thing we used to do in Las Vegas was watch the atomic bombs explode in the distance. There was a lounge at the Desert Inn with a huge wall of glass. You could go up there to sit and watch the bomb go off. First you would see the flash, the fire, then the mushroom cloud. Once, we even got in the car and drove away from the lights of the strip to get a better view. Nobody really knew the dangers of radiation and fallout at that time. In fact, the newspaper used to publish the radiation content in the milk every morning.

The United States government was exploding bombs in the desert 90 miles outside of Las Vegas frequently in the mid to late 1950's. There were lots of generals and military chiefs in all the hotels. I still don't understand how they could be doing all of this ten years after the war. How could they not have known what they were doing? And it was night after night after night, only 90 miles away!

So many people I worked with in Las Vegas have been dead for a long time. I thank God I'm still here. But later, I did get cancer on my face and in my body. I have never been a sun worshiper, but even if I were, I wouldn't have had the time. I worked at night and stayed in during the day. The melanoma that grew on my face had to come from somewhere and maybe those bombs were the cause.

Puerto Rico

New York and Las Vegas were certainly important to my career, but I took my act to cities all over the country, even Cuba and Puerto Rico. I opened three hotels in Puerto Rico, including The El San Juan and The Poinsettia.

I was married to Billy Condon when I opened the El San Juan and he came down to spend time with me while I was working there. During the day, we used to go to the old quarter in Old San Juan, which reminded me very much of the French Quarter in New Orleans, so I liked it a lot. There were so many little interesting shops.

At one place, there was a very good, self-taught painter who was quite prolific in many ways. He had ten children. This man had a friend who was a schooled painter who was also very good. His name was Domingo Garcia. I went to the gallery that was showing his work and bought a couple of his paintings. We suspected, after a few visits, that he was a communist. Don't forget, this was the height of the McCarthy era. But every time I asked him about his activities or his philosophies, he would just ignore me as if I was not there.

One day I asked him to come and see my show. He said he would be delighted to come. The next night, he came to the second show. Billy met him and took him to our table. Afterwards, we all went to a little restaurant for a bite to eat. After dinner, Domingo Garcia got very serious and said to me, "You have been trying to get me to tell you what my thoughts are and how I live. But since you were just another woman, I didn't pay any attention to you. But after seeing you perform, I now know that you are an artist. And as an artist, you have my attention. And now I will tell you what I do."

He then proceeded to tell us, "I am the head of the organization here in Puerto Rico to overthrow the government."

Impressed, I said, "Oh really!"

He went on to say that he was a communist, and the longer he talked, the more he resembled a wild man. His eyes got bigger and he got more and more excited. He told us he had three suitcases packed and ready to go at three different friends' apartments so if he needed to, he could escape the country very rapidly. Then he started talking about Fidel Castro. He said if Castro ever got too big for his britches, the communists themselves would annihilate him. Those were the orders from Moscow. Then, he started on George Washington and how terrible he was. He accused Washington of abusing his position because he was an entrepreneur, working for himself even as he was working for the people.

While he went on and on, we were all thinking he was terribly misinformed and very wrong. Finally, Billy got up, threw down his napkin and said, "I don't have to listen to this!"

I said, "Billy, sit down. If we don't listen to him, how will we ever know how they think?"

So he did and we let him talk. It was absolutely unbelievable. He was the leading artist in Puerto Rico at the time and I have often wondered what happened to him.

It was not long after that encounter that Billy and I sent out a Valentine card with an anti-communist statement in the greeting in the form of a poem he wrote. We were always sending out crazy cards for Christmas or New Year's. We got the whole family together, parents, kids, the children's nurse, Becky, and even our poodle, Dewey-Dewey.

One year, Billy put the baby, Marguerite, on a big silver venison platter in the middle of the dining room table and held the huge domed lid above her. Everybody around the table has surprised looks on their faces and inside the card, the caption reads: "May you also have many happy surprises in the coming New Year!"

Boston 1957

As a nightclub entertainer, I had to take my show on the road. Boston was always one of my stops on the supper club circuit, and I still have a following there. I took my first act to Framingham, where I met a young comedian who went on before me. He was a handsome boy who came from the Italian neighborhood of Boston near Federal Hill. One evening, he asked me to come to his uncle's house to meet his family. His uncle was a Sicilian wine maker and had been a devoted fan of mine from the days of *Your Show of Shows*. I told him I would be delighted to go.

This section of Boston was quite old and very modest, and the houses and apartment buildings still had no indoor plumbing. However, there was a public bath that the local residents used.

Everyone knew I was coming and they really prepared for me. The house had been scrubbed from back to front, and newspapers were put down on the floor so no one would mess it up before I came. When I arrived, everyone was thrilled, almost as if they were surprised I had actually shown up. I was offered a very nice red wine that had been opened just for me and we sat and talked.

After a little while, one of the neighbors came over, all dressed up, and said, "Oh, I just wanted to drop by and see how you were doing today." At that point, my host would invite them in and say, "Oh, by the way, this is Marguerite Piazza." I would say hello. They would stay for a few minutes, then leave. One by one, the whole neighborhood stopped by to use the telephone, or for another reason. It was quite an experience and I had a wonderful time playing along.

Miami Beach

I opened a lot of hotels in the fifties because there were a lot of grand hotels opening in those days. One was the Americana in Miami Beach. At that time, the Americana was considered way out in the boonies. I was two months pregnant with my son, Billy, and of course, no one knew. We were still doing The First Act, ending with the Dixie number. I had a banjo player, John Calli, who worked and traveled with me, who was just great. He played the mandolin during the Italian opening, the guitar during the popular songs and the banjo during the Dixie, and knew the act by heart.

The lead trumpet, always played by a local musician, was very important to the act. We had little sheets of music to mount on the instruments with holders, like a marching band, for the Dixieland finale and on opening night, I guess he was having trouble reading it. Since he was one of the four musicians who came out of the band with John Calli to march around the room, we had to get him up to speed. So, we rehearsed it and rehearsed it until we thought he had it.

Unfortunately, he didn't have it. When we got to the finale, he stood up and modulated to a foreign key, which almost threw everybody off, especially me. I don't know what would have happened if it had not been for John Calli. John knew the music inside and out and was so strong with his banjo that he just forced everybody into the right key.

When I came off the stage, I exploded. I told this man, "You can't be doing that on the stage. I mean, get this thing right. My God, you almost ruined the act." We rehearsed him again, but when we went out to do the second show, he made the same mistake. Well, at that, I went into orbit. I was such a perfectionist that anything that was musically incorrect really threw me. I just couldn't take it.

That night, a little after two in the morning, I was standing in the bathroom brushing my teeth, getting ready to go to bed, when all of the sudden, my insides seemed to drop out onto the floor. Shocked, I discovered that I was having a very serious hemorrhage. My Aunt Ann, who was always with me, flew into action. She put me in the bed and put a call through to Dr. Bringle in Memphis, Tennessee.

The hotel people didn't know I was pregnant, but since we were calling a doctor in Memphis who was delivering a baby, causing us to wait until he was finished, now the telephone operator and the whole hotel knew. They weren't as liberal about things like that back then. Even the Metropolitan Opera made me tell them when I was menstruating, when I first joined the company.

Finally, Dr. Bringle called back and said I would probably have a miscarriage. But he said he would send us some pills in the hopes that they might stop it. The only all-night drug store was in Miami, so the pills had to be sent by taxi across the causeway and way out on the island of Miami Beach to the Americana. My aunt then stood over me for twenty-four hours and gave me those tablets every hour.

I missed performing only one night. The comedian, Jerry Lester, went on for me. Jerry had been a host of the TV show, *Broadway Open House,* which ran for 15 months on NBC in 1950-51. It was the first network late-night show and a forerunner of the Tonight Show. The next night, I was back on stage doing two shows, dancing and doing my usual number. In those days, the show went on at any cost.

Being a perfectionist has its pros and cons. I was trained early on to work and polish my performance until it was as perfect as I could get it. And when it was so ingrained in me that I could do it at the drop of a hat, then and only then would it sound spontaneous. Only then was I completely free to do what I pleased with the interpretation. I enjoyed the feeling that I was in total control. And I loved what I was doing. But, to the local house bands in supper clubs, doing two shows a night often seemed a sort of hacking away to them. I could never accept this. When one note was played incorrectly, I heard it and it bothered me. I just had to have that perfect strand of pearls.

One night a week, on Sunday, we had a substitute orchestra. So, like the day I had arrived in Las Vegas, I would rehearse the new band in the afternoon and do two shows that night. That, again, was very hard.

Not long ago, I had my daughter, Marguerite, with me where I was doing a performance and we were up in my room before the show. The dinner was going on downstairs. Music was playing and people were having fun. But I was in my room busy getting dressed and being quiet. I said to her, "This is what it was like, every night, all the time I was in supper clubs. You'd think it was a glamorous life, the big shows, the great rooms, all the food, the champagne and the bands playing. But the singer has to take care of her body, because her body is the instrument. Other people have pianos to play, or violins or clarinets. But for the singer, the body is the instrument and it must be kept healthy and tuned up so you can go out there and use it. Play it. Do it."

However, the waiting was constant. When I was supposed to go on at 9 p.m., they often called me five minutes before to tell me they've just picked up the main course and now they're serving the dessert. It will be another 20 minutes, maybe a half hour. So, I'd wait. Finally, the phone would ring again and I'd have ten minutes to prepare. That's when I would go downstairs, catch my breath, and go on.

Cuba

After I finished my two weeks at the Americana, I was scheduled to open, without a night off, in Cuba. We had to pack all the costumes and scenery and also organize myself, my Aunt Ann, John Calli, and Willie Kaplan, the pianist, and get everyone and everything on the plane to Cuba.

When we got to the hotel, the first problem I faced was the light man. There were 85 light cues written out, in English of course. But the light man in Cuba did not read English, nor did he know anything about light cues. That threw me again.

Those were turbulent times in Cuba in the mid-50's. The communists already controlled the hotel, even though Cuba was still in the hands of the Batista dictatorship. This was just months before Castro took over. The maître d' of the room at the Hotel Nationale was from New York. While we were rehearsing, some friends of his from New York City came in to say hello. He invited them to sit and have a drink, and asked one of the waiters to bring some coffee.

The head of the communist union, who was in the room, came over to the maître d' and said, "What do you mean by asking these people in here to have a drink? You did not ask my permission for this. They will not be served and they can leave the room." This poor man, who in the normal chain of command would be running the room, had to put his tail between his legs like a dog and say, "I'm sorry, I can't serve you," to his friends from New York City. That was a big eye-opener for me.

Before the show, I was so upset with how bad the musicians were and how terrible the lights were that I had another hemorrhage. This was two weeks after the first one and I couldn't go on. My dear friend, Robert Merrill, and his wife, who plays the piano for him, were there and they sent word to me not to worry about a thing, they were going on for me. They did both shows, early and late, so I could stay in the bed.

Meanwhile, these gangster-like characters came up to my room with their big Cuban cigars to see what kind of a trick I was pulling and if I really was sick. They saw me in bed, unable to move, and I guess they assumed there was nothing they could do about it, so they let Robert Merrill go on. True to form, however, I was back on stage the next night.

Rebels were setting off bombs at that time to disrupt the city. They usually put a bomb near a junction box so it would knock out the power to an entire section of the city. One night, when Ann and I were having dinner in our room, a bomb exploded just outside the hotel. The force of it was so strong that it felt as if someone had pushed our heads into our plates. Before this trip, we had always thought of Havana as a very safe place. My Aunt Ann would even walk down the street by herself in the middle of the night to get sandwiches from a little deli not far from the hotel.

Now, there were Cuban soldiers stationed at the Hotel Nationale in Havana. They were at every door and elevator, and my son, Gregory, was fascinated by them. He used to love to watch the guards in their uniforms, guns at their sides, as they'd come to collect the money from the casino.

A few days later, my husband, Billy, joined us. After the last show, we all decided to go over to the Sansouci to hear Nat King Cole's late show. We were standing on the front steps of the Hotel Nationale when a big black limousine pulled up. Inside the car was a good friend of ours from Memphis with a lovely lady who was not his wife. The man saw us and the car took off, never coming to a complete stop. Billy thought that was hilarious.

Less than one minute later, another big black limousine pulled up and out stepped another friend from Memphis with a gorgeous redhead, also not his wife. He was so drunk, he didn't notice us until he actually brushed against Billy's sleeve going up the steps. He hesitated for a moment, and then decided not to say anything. But Billy couldn't stand it. He let them get to the top step before he said, "Hello so and so!" Embarrassed, the man stopped for another second, then he continued on without saying a word to us. Billy thought this was extremely funny, but I decided right then and there that Billy would never go on a "business trip" to Cuba without me!

The First Act lasted a little over two years, from 1955 to 1957. I took it all over the country. In two years, I could work everywhere twice, without having to change anything. But, after that, we gave it a major overhaul.

My son, Billy, was born in June, two months premature. He was supposed to be born on August 12th 1957, the day I was scheduled to open in Las Vegas. His very early birth was difficult, but he pulled through and I opened in Las Vegas on schedule.

The Wardrobe Fiasco

Two weeks after little Billy's birth, I flew to New York to work on the new act and to get the new wardrobe fitted. The popular and eccentric designer, Charles James, had already publicized that he was making three dresses for me that I would wear in my new Las Vegas show. I stood for hours while he had two dressers attend me. He pinned and he pinned and he pinned some more, all in muslin. We finally went to the French fabric house where he bought silks, bolt after bolt. I complained that he was buying everything in the house. His reply was, "Well, I don't know what I want yet." I paid him $3000 apiece for the dresses, in advance, and he was really cutting it close.

Finally, he promised he would have one ready for the opening and finish the others very soon after that. But I hadn't even seen a sketch of the dress. So I asked, "What's it going to look like?" He snapped back at me saying, "Have you ever seen a dress come out looking like the design?"

I said, "Maybe not exactly, but it will sure give me an idea of what it's going to be like." But, he never would draw the dress. I decided to get rid of this guy and get a new designer, but it was too late to hire anyone else.

I left for Las Vegas two days early so I could get used to the climate again, and get myself set up and ready to work. John Calli was coming out one day before we were to open. It was a Monday morning and he was supposed to pick up the dresses from Charles James at 7 a.m., then go to the airport to get on the plane and come to Las Vegas.

Well, at 5 a.m. Charlie called Raymond Katz on the phone, in tears. Alarmed, Raymond said, "What is it?"

Charlie said, "We've been working all night long on her dresses."

Raymond said, "Are they ready?"

To Raymond's amazement, he replied, "No, I didn't like it, so I cut it up."

Raymond said, "You did what!! That girl's not going to have a dress to open with tomorrow."

"Don't worry, I'll send something out there."

"But," Raymond said, "Keep in mind that it has to fit over the leotard. She can't have just any dress. It has to work in the act."

Charlie continued his weeping and then hung up.

There I was in Las Vegas with no clothes to wear for my act. I had to call Billy in Memphis, asking him to get my old black velvet dress, box it up and put it on the airline because I had nothing to wear. He did, but in those days, it wasn't easy. He had to pay a stewardess to take the box to Phoenix and give it to another stewardess who was coming from Phoenix to Las Vegas, as there was no direct flight from Memphis at that time.

At that point, I was prepared to go on stage in a bathrobe. Later, I told myself I should have done it--the publicity would have been fabulous! But my dress from home arrived two minutes before I was to go on, and I put it on instead.

To finish the costumes for the show, as he had promised, Charlie came out to Las Vegas, at my expense, with a young boy in tow, leaving his wife and two children back in New York. Temporarily, I put them in a little motel across the street from the Sands Hotel, where I was staying. Charlie didn't like that, he said he wanted to be at the Sands.

But the Sands was sold out, so I had to go to management and beg them for a room. Because it was me and because he was going to finish the costumes for the show, they put somebody else out and gave him a room. However, unbeknownst to me, Charlie cleverly put a briefcase in his room to show he was there, and then went across the street and stayed in the motel with his boyfriend.

While he was supposed to be working on the clothes, he failed to produce a single dress in a week's time. I became more and more uncomfortable about this, but pushed it to the back of my mind.

Then, the managers of the Sands came to me one day and said, "Miss Piazza, are you responsible for Charles James' bill here?" I said I was. Then the manager said to me, "Well, we want you to know that he has never been in the room."

I couldn't believe it! Charlie had had a tantrum because he didn't want to stay at the motel across the street, and now he'd chosen to stay there with his boyfriend! The manager told me the room was checked three times a day and the towels had never been used, the bed had never been turned down and there had never been a suitcase in the room. The only thing there was his little attaché case, which he didn't use.

Furious, I confronted Charlie with this when he came for the fitting. He threw the unfinished dress down at my feet and said, "I never wanted to do this dress anyway" and charged out of the room. At that point, I burst into tears because I knew I wouldn't have any clothes for my act.

I did have one unexpected champion. The captain of the room at The Sands, a very nice young man, had come to my dressing room to pick up Ann and myself, and take us to dinner at his home. I had just confronted Charlie, and he saw the state I was in. Coming over to me, he said, "Hey, Marguerite, you want me to take care of that guy? I can have some of the boys give him a hard time."

I said, "Oh, no. Leave him alone. Don't touch him. Let him go. He's not worth anything to me." The room captain was really going to take care of him! But I didn't want to be responsible for what might follow, although Charlie clearly deserved it!

For four weeks straight, I performed two shows a night in my one black dress. Even the management was talking about that black dress. They tried to get someone in L.A. to make a dress for me, but the dressmaker wanted me to fly to L.A. to fit it. The fog was very thick over the mountains and I didn't finish my last show until about 2 a.m. Yet they wanted me to get up at 5 a.m. to go to the airport and fly over those mountains in all the fog. That was where I drew the line.

This experience was one that I'd never forget, but the kindness of those who tried to help was something I'd also remember. And how could I complain? After all, I was in show business!

Recording

I loved the music of the great Broadway productions, so when I decided to make an album, we chose all the showstoppers from World War I through the 1950's. They were all great songs and show tunes, and I called the album "Memorable Moments of Music." We recorded it in an old club in New York. It was an all-wood auditorium and the acoustics were outstanding. I created the same variety on my record that I had in my act.

In addition to show tunes, I included two operatic arias on the album: the "Un Bel Di Vedremo" from *Madame Butterfly* and "Vesti La Giubba" from *Pagliacci*, which is really a man's aria. I always thought the tenors had all the best arias, and one day I decided that I wanted to sing a man's aria and I didn't care what the critics would say. So I did.

To really mix things up, I recorded "When the Saints Go Marchin' In." It was an unusual arrangement with a choral group and very few instruments. We also did a rendition of "Swing Low Sweet Chariot," an old African-American hymn.

The conductor on the album was very good with pop music, but the operatic arias threw him. I had wanted to hire Sylvan Levin, a classical musician, to come in and at least conduct the aria for me. But somehow, I couldn't put it together, to my regret. I didn't have quite the freedom in the "Un Bel Di" that I should have had. Why opera frightens some musicians, I'll never know. But it was a successful recording. Richard Rogers wrote the program notes on the back side of the album cover.

I suppose I've sung the "Un Bel Di" from *Madame Butterfly* more than any other performer who has ever lived. I sang it for about eight years in supper clubs, two shows a night. I got to where I could just push a button in my mind and the "Un Bel Di" would come out. It wasn't hard for me; in fact, it was an extremely easy aria for me and I loved to sing it. Most people might think an operatic aria would not go over in a supper club, but it did. I always set it up by telling the story before I sang it. By the time I finished with the story, I was in character and ready to sing.

I did the same thing for "Musetta's Waltz Song" from *La Boheme*. Setting it up properly made it fun for the audience. They knew every word I was saying, even though it was in Italian, because my gestures and expressions, along with the story I had just told, made it obvious.

The only other major recording I made was an album called "Marguerite Piazza Sings Torch" and it was very good. It started to take off in sales, but there was one thing wrong with it: I hated the picture on the cover. The photographer had wrapped me in a bath towel, which I didn't think was sexy at all. I looked as if I were sitting in a darkened room waiting to take a shower!

Finally, despite the public's obvious affection for the album, which was selling well, I pulled it off the market. That was one big fat mistake, as I lost thousands of dollars of potential sales income. It's a collector's item now and you would be hard-pressed to find a vintage copy.

Advertising and Cigarettes

At this point in my career, I had the opportunity to do a lot of ads. And I did. I advertised everything from Italian salad dressing to furniture and shampoo to maternity clothes. But the ad campaign that I got the most exposure from was for Camel cigarettes. I know what you're going to say. How could someone who has never smoked a cigarette in her life get in front of a camera and sell them?

Well, all I can say is, things were different then. We didn't know how bad they were. And everyone who was anyone had a cigarette ad. It was really fabulous publicity, so I did it. I made two TV commercials for Camel cigarettes. The first was just me sitting on a sofa in a lovely room, a coffee table in front of me. I had to pick up a cigarette lighter with my left hand, strike it with my thumb and light the cigarette, which of course, I didn't know how to do.

First of all, the cigarette lighter weighed a ton. It was one of those heavy glass ones of the day. Then, I found it very hard to light with my thumb, as I've never had a great deal of strength in my fingertips. And when I finally did get the lighter to work and took a puff of the cigarette, most of the time I convulsed, choking and coughing.

I was then taught how to draw on the cigarette without inhaling, and needless to say, they had to do a lot of takes. I think I went through a whole pack of cigarettes trying to light one. But we finally got one good take.

In 1988, there was a TV special on smoking that talked about how glamorous it had been to smoke in the 30's, 40's and 50's. They showed how movies glamorized smoking in romantic scenes, battle scenes, you name it.

And then they showed, of all things, an old ad of mine. There I am smoking a cigarette. In the ad I said, "When I smoke, I smoke a Camel." Of course! The only time I smoked was for the Camel commercial. As soon as that clip on TV was over, my phone rang and one of my children said, "Mama, what were you doing in that ad?"

I said, "Forget it. Your father didn't like it, either." But I advertised them for five years, the length of my contract.

I made one other television commercial where I was sitting in a doctor's chair. He was looking at my throat and saying, "There's no trace of any irritation due to smoking." Of course there wasn't. I didn't smoke. Shortly after making the commercial, the government banned ads using doctors and that particular one never made it from the editing room to the television set. But there were many, many still pictures taken of me for Camel.

Once, they took out a full-page ad in the New York Times showing me seated on the sofa with that heavy glass lighter and a lit cigarette saying, "When I smoke, I smoke a Camel." It was also on the back cover of a lot of magazines. In addition to the publicity, I received two cartons of cigarettes every week, which I gave to the people who worked for me. They were, of course, thrilled.

When it came time for me to sign a contract for another five years, I was married to Billy Condon. He said, "Absolutely not! That's false advertising. You don't smoke." And he sent my contract back to the R.J. Reynolds Tobacco Company. He was really angry with me over that. And yet he ran a snuff company!

The Second Act: 1957

When it came time to change the act, we hired Herb Ross again. His price had gone up considerably by then, but he was well worth it. Herb Ross was a brilliant choreographer and went on to become a highly successful director of over 30 feature films. My second act opened in nineteenth century Vienna, and I appeared in a beautiful white satin gown with a big hoop skirt. My neck and shoulders were bare, and there was a little puff of a sleeve at the top of my arm.

I entered with a dancer who was dressed like a prince. He wore a white outfit with silver epaulets on his shoulders and I sang the Blue Danube, Wein Barcarole, and all the Viennese Waltzes. It was absolutely beautiful and everybody loved it. But for some reason, they didn't applaud. I was used to really causing a stir and getting a crowd going. But I later realized that was the drawback to doing such a pretty, dream-like piece. People were so enchanted, they just did not burst into applause. Instead, because it was so beautiful and so relaxing, it lulled the audience into a peaceful state, which was nice for them. But when you're up there on stage, working very hard at what you're doing, you need enthusiastic applause. Ultimately, I couldn't stand it and dropped that part of the act. I just couldn't take the lack of response.

After the waltzes, the dancer reappeared with a big black cloak, which he swirled around and placed on the floor. I did a little striptease here and removed my shoes, my gloves, my jewelry and finally, I stepped on the cape, pulled the zip, unhooked the hook, dropped the heavy dress and stepped out of it. The dancer then closed it all up and carried it off.

So here I was, dressed in a black lace leotard and tights with ruffled pink pantalets over them. At this point, the dancer brought onstage a portable sitz bathtub and placed it behind a thin screen of fabric. With one good tug on the pantalets, they were off and then I disappeared behind the screen and got in the tub. A light then came on behind me, casting my shadow on the screen. It really looked as if I were naked!

While I "bathed," the dancer pretended to pour champagne from a huge bottle into my bath. And while all of this was going on, I was singing "La Danza," which is a great piece all in Italian with lots of high runs and trills. It was amazing that I could get it out at all, sitting in that tub. But this part of the act was a big hit.

After that, I appeared in front of the screen again, this time in my husband Billy's pajamas, which were enormous on me. I did a cute little dance with the dancer and then sang, "Let's Put Out the Lights and Go to Sleep." My finale was a rousing Gay 90's routine." (The black leotard I had on under the pajamas had a little bustle in back and I stuck a plume in my hair to give it a nineteenth-century flair. Then I did a few songs like "Hard Hearted Hanna," "A Good Man is hard To Find," and "See What the Boys in the Back Room Will Have."

We ended that act with "Shall we Dance" with the dancer picking me up, putting me on his shoulder, and carrying me off.

The second act was a three-ring circus. At times, it was almost more than I could keep up with. The scenery was packed in a big box that resembled a coffin. Each piece was numbered and documented as to where it had to go. My poor Aunt Ann, after we finished in New York where we premiered the show, took all night long with two stagehands to figure out how to get the scenery back in the box. She was so frustrated, she finally told me, "I'm not doing that again." That was a first! So we took it to California and used it one more time at the Coconut Grove. And that was the end of the scenery.

After I had warmed up the act a little, I took it back to the Hotel Pierre in New York, where I always opened each new act. While I was at the Pierre, I began to receive love letters every day from a middle-European man who never signed his name. We had no idea who he was. The reason they thought he was a middle-European, Hungarian or Rumanian, was because the letters were all decorated with hearts and little doves and flowers, in the artistic genre of middle Europe. We became afraid after a while that this man might try to find me alone or try to come after me, even though the letters were far from threatening. They were, after all, love letters.

Still, a man from hotel security would meet me at my suite and take me down to the room where I would be performing. After the show was over, he would take me back up to my room, go in and search it completely before I went inside. It was strange, but the guard I had was also middle European. He was Hungarian and, coincidentally, from the same little town in Hungary as the Gabor sisters. He enjoyed regaling us with amazing stories about the Gabors before they left that town and became stars in America.

Later, I had another incident in New York, this time at the Plaza. I had been engaged to do a few weeks there and my Aunt Ann and I had just arrived. We hadn't even unpacked our suitcases. We were in a tremendous suite with high ceilings and lots of rooms with enormous old doors and several entrances. There was a main entrance into the foyer, a back entrance from the days when people traveled with servants, and another entrance into the bedroom. There was no way to catch anyone in that place because it was so vast and so antiquated.

It was a Saturday afternoon and I went to the beauty parlor on Fifth Avenue at West 59th Street while Ann went shopping on Madison Avenue. We left at the same time, but Ann came back a few hours later. She put down her packages and went into my room for something. Suddenly, she noticed that things were scattered all around. She knew we hadn't left it like that, and the room had just been made up. It was in perfect order when we left.

Then she noticed the suitcases were open. Immediately, she called me at the beauty parlor to see if I had been back to the hotel since she had been gone. I said no and Ann said, "I think we've been robbed." She immediately called management and they sent up the detectives. The manager came up with them and they all thought it had to be an inside job. They called the 18th Precinct and said Marguerite Piazza had been robbed. Before long, there must have been a dozen detectives who showed up at the same time.

The detectives examined the door and said it was definitely not an inside job. Someone had carved the wood around the lock so they could force it open. They could see shavings all over the floor.

118

Furthermore, hotel guests didn't have to collect their mail from the desk. At the Plaza, they would bring it up and wedge it into the groove of the door.

When Ann had come in, she hadn't noticed the wood shavings, but she had seen the mail scattered on the floor. The robbers got away with a lot of my things, mostly jewelry. But they also took a mink coat and one of Ann's suits with a mink collar. Since the burglars took over $5,000 worth of goods, the FBI was brought in. When Raymond found out about it, he said "Don't give it to the papers. We don't want any bad publicity for the hotel. They'll never have you back."

I did keep it a secret. Two weeks later, Eartha Kitt was playing the Plaza and the same thing happened to her. However, she took advantage of the publicity. It was all over the front page! And guess who was back at the Plaza first? Eartha Kitt.

The publicity people for the Plaza came to my rehearsal that afternoon and took a photograph of me resting between numbers, dressed in the black leotard and tights with a cup of coffee in my hand. It's a very dark picture and is all face and legs. The picture made a full page in the New Yorker Magazine and the poster was also in the lobby of the Plaza while I was there.

When I was working the Plaza, the general manager was a man named Neil Lang. He was a powerful man who ordered everybody around and ran a very tight ship. If there was a light out in the marquee, he knew about it and had it taken care of immediately. While I was there, they were in the process of redoing an entire floor, and Neil Lang took me up there to see the work they'd done.

Everything had been stripped down to the concrete, and they were starting over from scratch. I thought I had instigated a few major repairs in my lifetime, but the scale of this was mind-boggling. The Plaza was very much in need of repair in the 1950's and, after seeing that, I can not imagine the scale of renovation that Donald and Ivana Trump took on with The Plaza when they owned it.

It was always a joy to work for the top hotels in the country, because everything was done with such perfection. Mr. Lang was very accommodating and always saw that I had everything I needed. I asked him for a refrigerator once so I could keep some food in my suite. And, of course, up came this huge thing, which they put at one end of the living room. I had to put a screen in front of it, it was so big. But when I opened it, I realized that he had also filled it with Dom Perignon champagne for me. What a sweet gesture that was!

Judy Garland

One of the most interesting and fun things about being an entertainer is that you never know who you're going to meet. Once, when I was playing the Plaza, I got a call from Judy Garland. We had never met, but she said she had seen my show and would like to come up and have tea with me. I said, "Wonderful, come on over." She arrived with her two children and we all had the loveliest afternoon together. It's funny when I think about it, but we were like two matrons having tea together.

The best part of the afternoon was that neither of us mentioned show business. We had a good time just talking about our children and our homes and domestic matters. Judy was such a genuine, warm and down-to-earth person, I only wish I had known her longer.

My Two Months as a Blonde

About two years after I started doing my act, I went to the beauty parlor one day and the hairdresser said to me, "Why don't you let me make you a redhead?" I thought about it for a few seconds, and then said, "OK."

She proceeded to dye my black hair red, but I found it terribly inconvenient. If you're a redhead, you just can't wear certain colors. As a brunette with ivory-colored skin, I had always been able to wear any color I pleased. Everything, of course, looked good over black and white.

So I went back to the beauty parlor and said, "Listen, I can't wear my clothes with this red hair. Can we do something else?"

She said, "OK, I'm going to make you a blonde."

This was in Memphis and we were living on Walnut Grove Road. My mother was visiting at the time and when I came home from the beauty parlor as a baby blonde, she disliked the new look intensely. In fact, when I walked into the kitchen, she stopped doing what she was doing, took a good look at me and said, "Darling, you know I love you, don't you?"

I said, "Sure, Ma, of course I know you love me. But what do you think about my hair?"

"Well," she said, "Let me be the first to tell you. If you think that you've done yourself a favor, you have not." And that's the way I began my two months as a blonde.

I went to Chicago to perform at the Chez Paris Club and Shecky Greene was my opening act. I remember that very well because he did a whole bit about an opera singer and how funny the opera singer was. For some reason, this didn't sit well with me at all. This was when I was still doing my first act and I guess I must have looked a little silly all dressed up in Italian Columbine regalia with a head of platinum blonde hair. But I did my show, and soon afterwards, I began to receive notes backstage from people who came to see the show saying, "You are not the girl we came to see. What happened to your black hair?"

I got so many of these notes from people objecting to me being a blonde that one afternoon I went to Helena Rubenstein's salon and said, "Can you make me a brunette this afternoon?" They dyed my hair back to its original color and I went on that night, once again as a brunette. What a relief! Being a blonde with my hair as dark as it was, I had to bleach it every five days to keep from having a black halo around my face. It was a tremendous chore that I thoroughly disliked.

The Kennedys and the Leotard

In the late 1950s, around the time I took my second act to New York, I met a wonderful couple who would become close friends, Teddy and Marion Donahue. I went to do a benefit at their Catholic church in Connecticut and stayed with them in their home. In fact, Teddy is my daughter, Marguerite's, godfather.

Teddy Donahue had gone to school with Steven Smith, who married Jean Kennedy. When the family decided to launch Jean Kennedy Smith into New York society, they gave a huge benefit ball. It was the First Annual Ball for the Mentally Disabled, and Teddy Donahue was in charge. My husband, Billy, and I were there as guests and Sammy Davis, Jr. performed.

The theme was the Wild West, and everyone was dressed in turn-of-the-century clothes. Billy dressed as Bat Masterson and I wore the black lace leotard from my second act with the plume that gave it a turn-of-the-century look. I carried a little feather muff, and the only thing on my legs was a pair of black stockings. I was actually two months pregnant, but it didn't show.

Jack and Jackie Kennedy were there. He was a senator at the time and they walked all the way across the room to meet "the girl in the leotard."

A few years later when Senator Albert Gore, Sr. asked me if I would sing for the First Congressional Wives Luncheon for the new president's wife, Jackie Kennedy, I said I would be happy to. The day of the luncheon, we had to wait about an hour for them. They were in Canada meeting with Pierre Trudeau, and were late getting back to Washington. But the entire assemblage just sat and waited until they arrived.

Finally, Jackie came in and I gave my performance. We were talking afterwards and she suddenly said, "I remember you. You're the one in the leotard!" I said, "That's right!" Although it was a strange way to be remembered, it was a link between us.

The Russian Bear

One of the most unlikely places I performed was at a party in Pittsburgh. There was a very rich couple there who had been in an automobile accident, which had put them out of commission for about a month. She was one of the wealthy Mellons.

After they recovered, they decided to have a big party for a hundred of their friends from all over the country. They sent planes to pick everybody up and they sent one to get Billy and me in Memphis. They also brought in Stanley Melba and his band from the Hotel Pierre in New York City. They knew I had been working The Pierre in those days and wanted their orchestra to be with me. They had also engaged a circus act to go on first.

Well, this was the most glamorous party you've ever seen, with everybody dressed to the nines. I've never seen so much exquisite jewelry. The guests were seated for dinner and the champagne was flowing when the first act appeared. It was a huge Russian bear that rode a bicycle and did some other tricks.

The trainer, of course, had a muzzle on the bear, but the animal went a little too close to one of the tables and knocked over a glass of champagne. When some of it got on his paw, the bear licked it and decided he liked it very much. At that point, he turned and went for the table. You've never seen a room empty so fast in all your life! The table went, the champagne went and the guests went. Finally, the trainer got control of the bear and led him out.

When they finally restored order and supper had been served, I had to come out and do my act. Talk about having a hard act to follow! My husband, Billy, knew quite a few people there and we were up until dawn, sitting on the staircase of the Rolling Rock Club singing songs that I would blush to repeat. It was great fun!

Chauncey the Cougar

When you're doing publicity, you are sometimes at the mercy of extraordinary circumstances. Sheriff Buford T. Pusser (made famous in the 1970's by the movie, "Walking Tall") and I were doing a promotional spot in Memphis, sponsored by the makers of Cougar automobiles. They wanted us to pose next to the car with a real, live cougar sitting on top of it.

Now, it's one thing to work with animals, but to work with wild animals can be really frightening. This big cat was a beautiful animal named Chauncey. He was the one who did all the TV commercials for the car, and they told me he was rather old and very tame and not to worry. Well, Sheriff Pusser was on one side of this big cat and I was on the other, and we posed for that picture very quickly and departed even faster.

But Chauncey wasn't my most frightening animal encounter. That one had occurred several years earlier, back in 1951, and her name was Ruth.

Riding Ruth

Sitting on my dressing table is a silver cigarette box, engraved, "In appreciation for your performance at NBC's 1st Annual Convention, Boca Raton Florida, December 1951." That box doesn't tell nearly the story of my first encounter with an elephant up close and very personal.

It all began when Sid Caesar and Imogene Coca were supposed to go to Boca to perform, but Imogene refused to fly. At his wit's end,

Max asked me if I would please go instead. "Oh, and besides performing that night," he said casually, "would you mind riding an elephant into the circle at the Boca Raton Club?"

"Sure, why not?" I replied. They told me to wear a bathing suit, so I put on my swimsuit and a pair of high heels and walked down to the pool to meet "Ruth" and her trainer.

I remember that it was a little before noon because just after they broke for lunch, I was supposed to ride the elephant in. Ruth was sitting down on the ground when I got there, so I had no idea how big she really was. They showed me how to sit on her neck, behind her head, and hold onto the leather strap. So, I took off my robe and got on. I held onto the strap when the trainer said "Up, Ruth!" and she started to stand up.

I thought she never would stop getting up as I went higher and higher and higher. That took me by surprise, but the trainer kept saying, "Don't worry about a thing. I'm going along with you and Ruth is a very docile elephant. Just hold onto the strap." And I did...for dear life! I held on until my knuckles were raw and clung to Ruth's neck with my legs. The tender skin on my legs was completely scratched up from Ruth's very rough skin. How those girls ride the elephants in the circus, I'll never know. Maybe they have special stockings on, but I didn't and it was tough.

At noon we rode in and Ruth had a big sign on her side that said, "NBC gives you more for your dollars" and everybody cheered. Finally, someone helped me down, but then they wanted to take pictures of me with the elephant. They told me, "Ruth is going to stand on her hind legs and we want you to run in, count 1-2-3-4 while we snap the picture, then you can run out." Well, I did it and lived to tell about it, but it's not something I would ever care to do again, thank you very much.

In Memphis for NBC 1953

Marguerite and Billy Condon 1953

Becky with the Children

Ray Katz and Marguerite with Barbara Walters

The Guy Mitchell Show 1957

The First Act – Italian Costume

The First Act – The Gown

The First Act – The Dixieland Outfit

Marguerite with Richard and Pat Nixon

Marguerite with Jackie Kennedy

Wearing Norell's Second Skin 1965

Caesar's Palace 1967

Marguerite with Doris Day

Marguerite with Phyllis Diller

131

1965

Marguerite with James Cagney

Marguerite with Rock Hudson and Bob Newhart

Valentine Card 1963

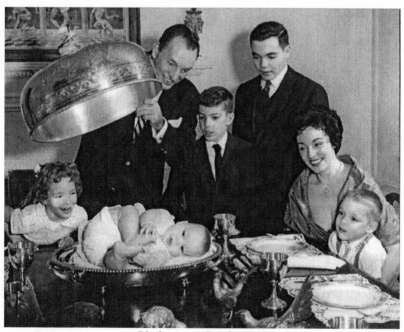

Christmas Card 1960

Part Five

The Third Act: 1959

About every two years, I completely changed my act, but I also made little adjustments along the way. I would take out a song here and add a new song there, just enough to keep it fresh and up to date. There were two very talented and wonderful individuals who created my third act, Lyn Duddy and Jerry Bresler. Once again, we opened with an Italian segment. I appeared on the stage in a colorful Italian peasant costume, carrying a tambourine with ribbons dangling from it. I opened with an energetic "I love a great big Italian Spozolizzio," followed by a medley of Italian folk songs which included "Come Back to Sorrento," "O' Marie," and "Ciribiribin." It was upbeat and fun and really got the audience warmed up.

I had, by now, become known for my quick and very entertaining costume changes, and this one would be no less dramatic. Underneath the Italian peasant dress, I had on a very special sequined sheath with long sleeves. The Italian dress was knee-length with a full ruffled skirt and only a string held up the long dress hidden underneath.

When I walked off the stage, I pulled down the zipper in back, the Italian dress fell to the floor and I stepped out of it. One pull on the string and the long gown went to the floor. Three seconds after my exit, I walked back out on stage totally transformed from Italian peasant to sleek, sexy siren.

It was so fast and such a dramatic change of appearance that the audience didn't think it was me. I loved the shock value and the response from the audience. What a great effect!

Norman Norell, the great American fashion icon, had designed my sequined sheath. He was the only American designer to challenge the supremacy of the Europeans of the time, like Coco Chanel and Christian Dior. He called this dress his "second skin" and that's exactly what it looked like. Thousands of sequins had been hand-sewn onto what was really a spandex-like tube from the neck to the floor.

135

I also called it my "mermaid dress." It was elegant and beautiful and a radical departure from the typical 1950's gown. But most of all, it was functional. If I wanted to spread my feet or dance or go down on one knee and bend to the floor with the microphone, it became very sexy, clinging to me as I moved. It was literally a glittering second skin.

I had the opportunity to meet Norman Norell several times and liked him very much. I never throw anything away and I still have a substantial collection of his designs, which I've even sent to various shows around the country. I loaned seventeen pieces to a retrospective of Norell's work at the Metropolitan Museum of Art in New York City in the early 1980's. He was still alive and was to receive an honor that night. But he had a stroke two days before and was unable to attend the ceremony. He died a few days later. His passing was a great loss to American fashion and design.

Later, in the 1990's, someone convinced me to sell one of those fabulous Norell dresses through an auction house in Los Angeles. It was a cobalt blue sequined sheath. A few months later, I saw a photo of Demi Moore wearing it in Vogue Magazine!

Lyn and Jerry wrote a very special song for my third act. I mentioned once that I collected lullabies and liked to sing them to my children before they went to sleep. So, they wrote the most beautiful lullaby called, "Hush-a-bye Baby." In the middle of all the popular music and show tunes, I sang it to the audience from a chair very close to the front tables. Everyone just loved it.

Before we opened the third act in New York, I took it to Boston to break it in for about three days. We were doing the show in this big barn of a place called Blinstrob's, which could seat a thousand people for dinner. My regular pianist, Willie Kaplan, couldn't go to Boston, so I engaged a new piano player/conductor.

The man turned out to be a little crazy, and got worse with each day. He was extremely paranoid. On stage, I introduced him as my pianist, and he corrected me by shouting, "Conductor!" Uh, oh, I thought. I sense trouble coming my way.

By the third night, just before the last show, he grabbed me backstage and demanded his money. He wasn't supposed to get his money until after the show, but he was so crazed that I gave it to him. He must have needed it to buy some more of whatever he was on, because later, in the middle of my act, he came over to me and stepped into the spotlight, wildly waving his arms and saying "You see, I am the conductor!"

He was high as a kite. My Aunt Ann thought he was going to hit me and ran to get the two bouncers who walked out on the stage, picked him up bodily and carried him off. Cardinal Cushing was in the audience that night, which made me even more upset with that idiot. After they hauled him off, the trumpet player came down and conducted, but I still didn't have a piano player and once again, I was terribly upset when I came off the stage.

I once had a review in Variety Magazine that said I was "an opera star who knows how to please both the longhairs and the crew cuts." In fact, that's one of the things I love most about singing. I love being able to put on a show that has enough variety to keep everybody on the edge of their seat. Being a veteran of highbrow opera, I thought if I could present classical music to someone who had never heard opera and make people actually enjoy it, I had really achieved something.

But it was just as much fun to give a little jolt to the society matrons and the "crew cuts" with something like an unexpected strip tease.

Lyn and Jerry wrote new lyrics to the Richard Rogers song, "Zip," from Pal Joey. The mermaid dress, with long sleeves, had lots of zippers, one on each sleeve starting at the wrist and going up to the elbow, and then one down the back. I sang, "Zip...Zippers always do a lot for a gal." And I unzipped the right sleeve.

Then I sang "Zip...I know lots of ways to raise your morale." And I would unzip the left sleeve. Then I sang, "Zip...It was Gypsy Rose who gave me my start." And I reached back and unzipped the back of the dress. As it fell to the floor, I sang, "Zip...I just love interpretive art!" At that point, I ended up in a black lace leotard and the dancer brings me a top hat and a cane with rhinestones on the top and we did a little soft shoe.

Pretty racy, I know, but fun all around.

The Pagliacci Routine

One of the most dramatic things I ever did as part of my act was the Pagliacci routine. We created it in 1959, but I used it off and on for over a decade. I had always wanted to sing the aria, "Vesti La

Giubba," (which is a man's aria) and here was my chance. I had it staged so that it was an event, not just a song. To give you a bit of the story, the opera begins when a troupe of actors arrive in a small town. Their leader, Canio, is very jealous of his wife, Nedda, and warns everyone that he will not tolerate any flirting with her.

When Nedda is alone, the deformed clown, Tonio, tries to make love to her, but she chases him away with a whip. He is followed by a handsome villager, Silvio, who is more successful with Nedda. Tonio sees them together and out of revenge for being turned away, he goes to Canio and tells him about his wife's infidelity.

Canio is crazed with jealousy and almost kills Nedda when she refuses to tell him who this man was. Then, left alone on the stage, Canio confesses how he must prepare for his performance that night and act the part of the famous clown, Pagliacci, wearing a big smile, even though his heart is broken. Then, he sings the very sad "Vesti La Giubba," which means, "Put On Your Costume."

My good friend and choreographer for *Your Show of Shows*, Jimmy Starbuck, staged this aria for my supper club act and it was marvelous. After the big number with a dance routine in leotard and tights, I would go over to a small makeup table that was made just for this piece. (Incidentally, the table was built by a young man who has since become one of the biggest TV producers in America, Gary Smith. I paid him $2,500 to design it and he made it completely by hand.)

Then, I would put down my top hat and cane and say to the audience:

"Have you ever wondered what the theatre really is?"

A violin would begin to play as I lifted the edge of the table, and lights would come on as the table edge became a stand-up frame, locking into place and looking like a lighted makeup mirror. But there was no mirror, only a space so I could see through to the audience.

Sitting at the dressing table, I went on to say that theater is:

"...a carnival. Grand Opera. Punch and Judy."

While talking over the music, I reached under the table and changed into flat black slippers.

"It's all the same. For wherever there is make-believe and an audience..."

Almost unnoticed, I slid into baggy white clown pants.

"There, we have theatre."

There was a brief pause while the audience saw me fiddle with something on the table, and then bring my hand to my face. Then, to their amazement, I smeared a big swipe of dead white clown makeup across my face. The audience gasped as I quickly smeared it all over my face.

"It might be Mickey Mouse or Shakespeare…"

Looking into the non-existent mirror, I drew two arched brows with heavy black pencil.

"Garbo…"

Then I drew two tears, straight lines, one beneath each eye.

"Or Sir Lawrence Olivier. There's something for everybody…"

I'd then wipe my hands on a cloth.

"And they all come to this magic place in search of happiness."

Picking up the white, baggy clown shirt with three big black pompoms for buttons, I'd pull it on.

"But the most exciting moment of all, is when the lights go down"

I'd lean over to put a black skullcap over my hair, my face coming up slowly into a dead white spot light as I said very softly:

"And the curtain goes up"

For a final touch, I'd put a black ruff around my neck, now completely transformed from glamorous nightclub singer to tragic clown.

"And this, my friends, is a performer's greatest moment."

The music would begin again, very somber and I would sing:

Recitar! Mentre preso dal delirio;

Non so piu quel che deco e quel che faccio!

Eppur e d'uopo sforzati! Bah!!

Sei to for se un nom?

Here I'd let out a burst of bitter laughter and slam my fist down with a bang onto the little table. And then I would sing:

Tu se' Pagliaccio!

With emotion, I would get up and walk to the front of the stage. And now, with clown hat in hand, I would sing:

Vesta la giubba e la faccla infarina. La gente paga a …etc.

When I finished, the audience went crazy. I took my bows still wearing the dramatic face. Then I walked off. I came back, bowed again and turned my back to the audience. I leaned over, almost crouching and pulled a referee's whistle out of my pocket and blew it with all the breath I had left.

This sent a shock wave through the audience. And when I turned around, the band struck up "The Gladiators," that great circus theme song. I went back to the little table, sat down, put on red cheeks, a big smile, and a bright red fright wig and hat.

Again, I was transformed, and began opening up my bag of tricks. First, I grabbed a toy trumpet and pretended to play that. Then, I made lots of noise with a triangle and played the Bells of St. Mary's on the glockenspiel. This was all completely orchestrated. Next, the stage went black except for a spotlight, which cut off at my knee while I picked up an umbrella and started to mime a tightrope act.

As if that weren't enough, I then went to the back of the stage and picked up a huge bass drum that I strapped to my body like a drummer in a marching band. Then, I'd march all over the stage, banging first one side of the drum, then the other, back and forth to a very big orchestration of "The Stars and Stripes Forever."

This program just about caused a riot. Although I didn't sing a single note after the Pagliacci, I was on for several more minutes and it brought the audience back up and got them excited. The routine got me the same national publicity that the first act had gotten me. *Variety* devoted a whole page to it, and everybody was talking about it.

The Pagliacci routine was great, but it was difficult to execute because everything had to be perfect for it to work. It required split-second timing. And thanks to my Aunt Ann, she took care of all that for me. She set up the table and it had to be exact. The right shoe had to be on the right side and in the right place, the same for the left shoe. The ruff that went around my neck went around the leg of the table. That's where I reached for it and it had to be there.

The face paint had to be in the right place, the little mirror that nobody saw had to be in the right place, the cloth to wipe my hands had to be there. The coat had to be folded properly, so when I pulled it out, it fell open in a way I could put my arms right into it. The pants had to be folded just right, so when I picked them up at the top, they were front to back, in the proper position.

All those things had to be planned and executed with precision or it could ruin the act. My loyal, wonderful Aunt Ann did this twice a night for me.

We were doing the show in New Orleans at the Roosevelt Hotel once when Ann, my rock, got very sick with food poisoning, and I thought she was going to die. She was bleeding and vomiting and couldn't stop until she was totally dehydrated. The hotel doctor came to see about her and stayed with her, and sent one of the bellboys to the all-night drug store to pick up a prescription. He stayed with her all night, holding her hand and watching her. She was that sick.

While I was desperately concerned about Ann, I was so dependent on her to set up that act that I needed to find someone to fill in. It wasn't something I could just ask someone to do for me, as it had to be done just so. My friend, Maxine Messenger, happened to be visiting from Houston that night and volunteered to help. So, in between being sick, Ann wrote down exactly what had to be done so that the act could go on. Maxine was very nervous about doing it, but she did it and thank God she was there. I remember finishing the act and going straight upstairs to see if Ann was still alive. Thankfully, she'd survived!

Another time when I was doing this act, I got to the Pagliacci routine, went over to the table and sat down. When I lifted the lights on that frame, I thought it clicked into place, but when I slammed my fist down on the table during the laugh, it came crashing down on my nose. That steel frame, traveling very fast, cut the skin to the bone and knocked the wind out of me. Blood spurted out and I put the small washcloth that I had there to wipe my hands on, over the cut.

With my automatic and thoroughly ingrained "The Show Must Go On" mentality in play, I rose and went to the front mike to continue the aria. But when I took my hand and the washcloth away from my face, the blood squirted out again and I realized I couldn't continue.

By this time, my Aunt Ann saw it and was screaming to the orchestra leader, "Leon, get Marguerite off that stage, she's hurt!" So I said to the audience, "I'm sorry. I can't continue." And I left the stage. Everyone in the audience was laughing. They thought it was part of the act, until they saw the blood all over my face.

There was a big football game in New Orleans the next day, and that night many of the players and coaches were in the audience. One of the team doctors happened to be a friend of mine from Memphis. He came backstage and after examining me, he said, "If you were one of the players, I'd sew you up right here. But with your face, I suggest you go to the emergency room and get a plastic surgeon to take care of it. You'll have less scarring."

And that's what I did, under local anesthesia. Then I came back to the Roosevelt and did a second show – with stitches!

Ode to Billy Condon

My husband, Billy Condon, was one of the most attractive men God had ever made. He was physically beautiful and his body was perfect. One of his best features was his gorgeous legs. I remember a picture that was printed in the paper once. Billy's legs were in the foreground with a shot of a golfer through them. They were just perfectly formed, for a man.

Billy also had aristocratic features, beautiful hands and a special grace about him. He was also a very talented man. He played the piano and he was always full of fun.

Billy was great with children, and always had a story or joke or something funny to do or say--literally, the life of every party he ever went to. People around Memphis thought that if they had Billy Condon at their party, it was sure to be a success because he was going to liven it up. Everybody loved him.

He had an interesting background. His mother was from Nashville and his father was from Memphis. When Shirley, his mother, was about eighteen years old, she was going to finishing school in New York City and happened to be engaged to dime store magnate, Samuel H. Kress. Mr. Kress opened his first dime store in Memphis, but by this time was a pretty big tycoon. He was a lot older than Shirley, but he had given her a ring and she was going to marry him. He was just wild about her, and she was a beautiful thing with masses of red-blond hair.

Billy's father, Martin Condon, Jr., whom everyone called Buddy, came to New York City one day and looked up Mr. Kress, who invited him to go to the Metropolitan Opera with himself and his fiancée, Shirley Cummins. So, Buddy went. After the opera, they went to Sherry's for dinner. Sam Kress had a little upset stomach, so he ordered milk toast, while Buddy ordered caviar and champagne. Young Shirley was so impressed by the dashing young Mr. Condon that she ran off with him and sent Mr. Kress his ring back. This broke Sam Kress's heart and he vowed never to marry. He went to his grave never breaking that vow.

Billy's grandfather, Marin James Condon, Sr. was tall, thin and rather athletic, not to mention very successful. He became the youngest mayor of Knoxville Tennessee at 25 and began to collect snuff companies at the same time Mr. Duke, his friend, was collecting cigarette companies. He also owned gold mines in Mexico, until Pancho Villa took them over. He lost something like six million dollars overnight, which would be like losing many times that today.

During the Depression, snuff was more popular than cigarettes because a nickel can of snuff was an affordable pleasure, as were the movies. That changed, but the American Snuff Company, which Martin had founded, and Billy and his brother ran, continued to prosper and eventually diversify. After I married Billy Condon, the press had a field day with my new association with snuff. They even claimed I left little cans of snuff on music stands for the musicians in the band.

Billy loved to play. At college, he was a star football player and when I met him, he was a champion golfer. He also played tennis and in general, he was a good athlete in anything he tried. He was a wonderful dancer, too. Every woman wanted to dance with Billy and I must say that I really enjoyed it myself. Honestly, he was like Fred Astaire. He just sort of floated around the dance floor and carried you with him.

He was always very flattering. He greeted you with "Hello darling, how are you?" Not just me, all the ladies were "Darling" and "Oh, you look wonderful tonight". But then after he'd said, "Oh, darling, how are you" and "Yes, sweetheart" and "Dear," he would turn and ask me "Who was that lady?"

And I would say, "You big fake, you. You're calling her darling and sweetheart and you don't even know her name?" But he didn't care; all ladies were darling to him. That's the way he was and everybody loved him, men included.

Billy lived the genteel life of the Southern gentry. He thought, why should he go to Europe or any other place for that matter when he lived so well at home? No, he was happy to stay in Memphis. But, we did do some traveling because I liked it. And if I had a concert to do, he often went with me because he had such a good time.

Billy Condon was very particular about his appearance and especially about his clothes. He was very neat and nothing was ever out of place. I was that way, too. We wanted the whole house to be that way. But I had a habit that became one of Billy's pet peeves. When I took my stockings off at night, I immediately washed them and hung them over the side of the tub to dry. It was a simple thing I did for myself. But Billy just hated it. If he caught me doing it, he'd say "Marguerite, don't do that. Let the servants do it." He was really Old World, so I did my best to hide my habit from him.

When Billy and I went on a trip, he usually had more clothes than I did. He liked those two-tone wing tip shoes, and had to have the black and white, brown and white, tan and white, as well as all black, all white, black dress shoes, and patent leather evening shoes. He traveled with both full dress tails and tuxedo.

I used to say to him, "Billy, I really don't think you need that on this trip."

"Oh, yes," he'd say. "I have to take them because you never know when you'll need them." The truth of the matter was, he grew up with that kind of clothing. He was comfortable in it and he liked to wear it, just as I am comfortable in evening gowns.

On Dressing Up, and Oscar

Speaking of evening dresses, they have been my work clothes forever and I am really most comfortable when I am all dressed up. That's just me. For years, I couldn't buy a dress to go to the grocery in because the salespeople simply would not allow me to do it. I would walk into a store and the first thing they would say was, "Oh, Miss Piazza, we have this wonderful evening dress that has just come in. You've got to try it on."

And I would say, "But all I want is a little everyday dress."

And the reply I would get was, "Yes, we'll find that for you later, but come try this evening dress on."

And that's the way it was. Finally, when they came out with good catalogues, I used to buy my everyday clothes through the mail because that was the only way I was sure to get them.

To be perfectly honest, I must admit to being a clotheshorse, too. There was a very dear lady in Memphis named Laclede who had the only real couture dress shop in Memphis for many years. It was a very small, exclusive and expensive boutique, which she called simply "Laclede's." The owner, Laclede, loved me, and when she went on her buying trips, she bought for me. It was she who introduced me to the clothes of Norman Norell, and while his "second skin" evening dresses were a knockout, Norell's daytime collection was just as wonderful. He made the most fabulous suits and I really enjoyed wearing his American designs.

I was always one to have a little fun with my clothes, especially accessories, like hats, handbags and even jewelry. I was performing in Houston when my friend Maxine Messenger told me about a certain kind of bug from Mexico. They were live beetles with hard, crusty shells. Semi-precious jewels had been attached to their backs and they were kept alive on a piece of balsa wood, in a little box. A gold chain was attached to the edge of the shell with a gold safety pin at the other end of the chain. You could pin it on your dress and there it would sit. Every once in a while, it would walk around your dress like a dog on a leash. It couldn't go any farther than the chain would allow, which was only three or four inches long. So, I bought one. I think I paid $600 for it. The stewardesses were smuggling them into the country, and they were making a bundle on these beetles.

I called my little bug, "Oscar," and I remember wearing it to a party at Justine's Restaurant in Memphis. Of course, everyone there was drinking. I didn't say a thing about the bug that was just pinned on my dress. Finally, a friend of mine said, "How do you get that thing to do that?"

I said, "What thing?"

And he said, "That mechanical thing you have on your shoulder. How are you working it?"

"Oh," I said, "That's Oscar. He's alive."

Well, the man just couldn't imagine that I had a real live, creepy crawly thing walking around on my dress. People just couldn't believe it. The expressions on their faces when they saw this bug crawling around, especially if they'd been drinking, were hilarious. I had a whole lot of fun with Oscar.

One day, Billy and I went to Nashville for a big summertime party, and it was very, very hot. I took Oscar out of his little box to put him on me, and realized that he had died. At the time, I Just couldn't understand why, but I later learned that I was supposed to soak the balsa wood in water every once in a while and I hadn't. I was so sad over that funny little beetle dying. I still have Oscar in his special little box in my dresser drawer.

Soon after that, the phone rang and a voice said "Miss Piazza?' I said yes. He said, "This is the FBI." I couldn't imagine why the FBI would want to talk to me. But they wanted to know where I had gotten my beetle.

I said, "What are you talking about?"

He replied, "Did you know that it is against the law to bring beetles from Mexico into the United States? There is a tremendous fine for it and it's possible that you could go to jail!"

"What?!" I screamed. "Yes, Ma'am, and we want to know where you got it."

I said that I was working in Houston in a supper club and someone gave it to me. He asked who and I told him it was just a fan. He asked me where my bug was, and I told him Oscar had died, which was the truth. So, he scolded me and told me never to do anything like that again. And believe me, I haven't. But I can't help but wonder if the FBI still has a file on me for the illegal possession of a bug!

Life with Billy Condon

When NBC sent me to Memphis in 1953 to save the NBC station from being bought out by CBS, I had been Graves' widow for six months. I arrived in Memphis during the Cotton Carnival, and my friends (Graves' relatives), Percy and Jodie McDonald, selected Billy Condon to be my escort. Billy graciously accompanied me the entire time. We were up almost twenty-four hours a day going to various functions.

We attended every party there was in Memphis for the Cotton Carnival. Finally, on that last night when he brought me back home, it was about four o'clock in the morning. I had to leave a few hours later to return to New York and *Your Show of Shows*. Billy said goodnight and that he'd had a great time. Then, he turned and left me standing in the middle of the living room, went to the door, opened it and started to go out.

But, Billy Condon made a decision, right then and there that would affect the rest of his life and mine, too. Instead of going out that door, he closed it, turned, came back into the room, took me into his arms and kissed me. My knees went weak and I fell in love with him right there on the spot.

Very little time passed before he came to see me in New York. Then I came back to Memphis to see him and we decided to get married. That was the beginning of my residence in Memphis. Oddly; I had never even been to Graves McDonald's apartment in Memphis until after he died, and I only went there to close it.

Memphis has been very good to me and I have enjoyed my time there. I have worked for Memphis and the city has worked for me, but it was difficult for my career. If I had been living in Los Angeles or New York, I would have been more active because I would have been on call for anything, such as TV shows and other things for which they pay scale. These are very important as far as publicity is concerned. But living in Memphis, it seemed hardly worthwhile to spend a small fortune for a round trip ticket and a hotel (not to mention the time) to do a job that paid scale of $149.50.

But living in Memphis was wonderful for my children. It was a much smaller town than L.A. or New York and I got along very well here. I had good help, too, which enabled me to go to work in clubs and stay away for two or three weeks at a time and still feel that my family was safe and well cared for.

And, of course, Billy was here. I wouldn't have cared if I was on the moon, as long as I could be with him, because I loved him so much. When I moved to Memphis after I married Billy, I brought my two sons, Gregory and Jimmy, with me. Billy legally adopted them and they both took the name Condon. Billy was always very good to them, but he didn't involve himself in their lives as much as he perhaps should have, such as taking them with him to play tennis and do all the things young boys should do. One day I found a note Gregory had written. It read, "My mother is married to a man who has no idea how to be a father to a boy." Billy was very much geared into a social world of his own. That was his passion in life.

But then, he was always very sweet to the boys. Becky, the children's nurse, told me a story about Billy being dressed up in his tuxedo, getting ready to go to a big party one night when I was out of town. Gregory asked him if he would come and say prayers with him and Jimmy, and he said, "Of course. I always have time to say prayers with you boys." So Billy got down on his knees in his freshly pressed tuxedo and prayed with those children. The boys addressed Billy as "Daddy" and he was the only Daddy that either one of them ever knew.

Some time later, when I was playing the Maisonnette Room in New York, Karl Kritz's first mother-in-law, Mrs. Goldsmith, called me. It was just before I was to go on the stage and she said, "Where is Gregory? His father just died and we'd like for him to go up to Syracuse with us for the funeral.

I told her I would call him and tell him. Then I went downstairs, did my show, came back up and really thought about it. I had already called Gregory, who was living in New York then, and said to get ready to go to Syracuse because your father has died. But I called him back and said, "Unpack! You're not going to that funeral. That man wasn't your father. Billy Condon was your father and the only one you ever knew. He took care of you, did everything for you and you're not going to that funeral."

Gregory didn't really know Karl Kritz from Adam. He met him once when he was eighteen years old, and somebody had said, "Gregory, this is your father." They shook hands and Karl had said, "How do you do." That was it. He never called or wrote to ask about Gregory and he never paid for any schooling, clothing or anything else. Nothing at all. Never. He had no influence on him whatsoever.

I had only known Jimmy's father, Graves McDonald, for two years when he died. So he had no influence on those boys, either. Billy Condon was their father.

When I moved to Memphis in 1954, it was in a dry county. Liquor was not sold by the glass, anywhere. So, Billy and I kept a locker at the country club stocked with whatever liquor or wines we wanted to serve when we entertained. Later, a voter referendum changed all that and people didn't have to "brown bag" their liquor when going out in Memphis. But, if we were going to Justine's, which was Memphis' only really fine French restaurant at that time, we had to bring whatever we wanted to drink along with us.

Billy really did not want that law changed, because he brought his good scotch or his good vodka and he knew what he was getting. But it was very inconvenient, especially for people who did not belong to clubs where it was taken care of for you.

Billy played the piano very well and he liked to play songs like "Pennies from Heaven" and "Shine On, Harvest Moon." We all sang together, with the family or with friends. One year, we had a Christmas card made up with the whole family gathered around the piano, with each child holding an instrument, and everyone singing.

Billy also loved to play and sing a particular barroom song called "St. James' Infirmary." When my daughter, Shirley, made her First Holy Communion, I had a breakfast for all sixteen of the little girls in her communion class. They all came across the street from the cathedral in their white dresses and veils. Our wonderful Becky had prepared bacon and eggs and sweet cakes and juice and all those good things. Then, after we finished with breakfast, we realized we still had an hour to go before their mothers would be there to collect them. So, we all went into the living room and decided to tell stories. When we were finished with that, we still had time left, so Billy said, "I'm going to play the piano." And he proceeded to play "St. James' Infirmary," leading all these sweet little girls in singing this pub song at their First Holy Communion breakfast! It was really hilarious. I can only hope they didn't go home and say, "This is what we learned at the Condon house."

Billy used to go to a little bar in the neighborhood called Huey's and I couldn't get him out of that place. One day, I asked him "What's the big attraction?"

He said, "They have an organ there, and when the guy goes on his breaks, they let me play the organ and I have a good time."

I said to myself, *I can do something about that.* So I called a friend of mine, Ethel Smith, who was a great organist and asked her how I should go about getting an organ. She said, "I have an extra one with all my special stops on it and I'd be glad to sell it to you." I paid $4000 for that organ, had it shipped to Memphis and gave it to Billy for Christmas. He was very happy with it. In fact, he played it a lot for awhile. But before long, he was back at Huey's.

I said, "Billy, I bought you the organ so you could have an organ to play all you want at home. Why are you going back to Huey's?"

He said, "You forgot one thing."

I said, "What did I forget?"

He said, "You forgot to buy the audience."

Party Time in Memphis

Billy and I sure had a lot of fun in Memphis. The Cotton Carnival and all the parties connected with it became a regular, yearly event for us. Our very dear friends from New York, Marion and Teddy Donahue, came to Memphis for a party called "The Mad Hatter's Ball." In honor of Billy's new business venture, Hot Shot Bug Spray, they brought a hat for Billy to wear (Teddy owned the company that made Talon zippers and one of his very creative employees made it.) It was a huge straw hat with a very wide brim and mosquito netting draped over it with big rubber bugs and spiders all over it.

Standing up around the top of the hat were several cans of Hot Shot, each a different formula. The veil of net with all the bugs in it hung down around his face. What a sight! The hat was a huge hit.

At the end of Carnival Week, there was always The Rebounder's Party. It was a costume party and usually more fun than any of the rest of Carnival. It always took place on the afternoon of the last night of Carnival in a different place every year, usually at someone's house. One year, we even had it at our house.

But this particular year, it was at the Memphis Hunt and Polo Club and we were out to win the prize for the best costumes. Billy hired a flatbed truck and we put an old claw-footed bathtub on it. I was dressed in my pink leotard from my act, and all you saw were my bare legs and arms sticking out of the tub. We had pink balloons all over me, rising up from the tub like bubbles.

Teddy was dressed as a butler, Marion as a French maid and Billy like a bartender. Well, we came down the road on this truck with Teddy holding up a huge bottle of champagne as if he were pouring it into the tub. I thought for sure we would win first prize, but somebody beat us. I wish I could remember what they had done--it must have been even more outrageous than our act!

The partying and drinking was a lot of fun, but occasionally, things got out of hand. One summer evening in the late fifties, Billy and I had gone to Mississippi for dinner. On the way home, we stopped at the dog track just across the river in Arkansas and Billy gambled away all the cash he had in his pockets. On the way home, we ran out of gas right at the approach to the old Mississippi River Bridge. The only money we had was one dollar that I happened to have in my purse.

We were both dressed to the hilt, not to mention my diamonds and pearls.

Well, we stood by the side of the road with our thumbs out for what seemed like ages, but no one would stop. Finally, a truck stopped and took us to the nearest gas station. It just so happened that we bought gas there and even had an account for our Dunbar Trucking Company. But the manager of the little station wasn't there, only a young boy who didn't know us and would not give us a container of gasoline.

Billy thought if he could get to the Peabody Hotel, they would cash a check for him. So I gave my one dollar to the truck driver to drop us off at the Peabody. We must have been a sight to see, all dressed up in our fancy clothes and jewelry. Here I was a TV star, climbing out of the cab of an 18-wheeler at the front door of the only five star hotel in the South because no one would trust us for a little can of gasoline. We finally cashed a check and got a taxi to take us back to the gas station and across the bridge to our car. No, there was never a dull moment with Billy Condon.

The House That Owned Me

The house that Billy and I bought on Central Avenue was a source of great joy for me. I lovingly transformed it from a big, empty, barn of a place into our comfortable, beautiful home. Much later, after Billy died, I had a beau in Los Angeles who wanted me to give up my life in Memphis and move to California. But I just couldn't give up my house. I had a love affair with my glorious house at 1720 Central Avenue. It was mine and I owned it. And it definitely owned me.

I put so much love and energy into making that house what it was that it had become a symbol for me, a place where all my dreams had come true. To me, it seemed that to part with that house meant parting with my dreams. I had convinced myself, when we first moved in, that my life was as close to perfect as anyone's life had ever come. I had the perfect career, perfect husband, perfect children, perfect house, perfect life, and I didn't want anything to change.

But, of course, nothing in life that is real is perfect. And nothing ever remains the same for very long. However, for many years, that house was the receptacle of my hopes, my dreams and my collection of beautiful things.

For the Love of Antiques

Very early in my career, when I was still a student and working with the New York City Opera, I began to make a little bit of money-- actually, a very little bit of money. My first publicist was a woman from New Orleans named Muriel Francis. Muriel loved antiques and was quite a buyer.

One day she took me shopping on the East Side, where there were lots of little antique shops. There was one place in particular called "Old Versailles" owned by two little French ladies. Muriel said this was one of the finest shops in New York City, and she was right. You could get things in this little shop that didn't exist in any other shop.

The day we went to see them, the two women were very upset. They didn't speak much English, but we figured out that one of their dear friends needed to raise some cash for an urgent crisis. As a result, they needed to sell the friends' two chairs that very day. The chairs were wonderful, and the ladies insisted they had come from the Petit Trianon of Marie Antoinette, but, of course, there were no papers.

Muriel looked at me and said, "Buy them!"

"Oh," I said, "I don't think I can. I don't think I have that much money."

Muriel insisted, "Buy them! If they say they are genuine, then they are. I have never known them to lie and I have bought a lot of stuff here." So I bought them for a staggering $100 apiece!

The first thing I did when I got home was to call my mother in New Orleans and have her cover that check for me. I still have the chairs and they are definitely of the period, as they said. But it is a great source of mystery and fun to think that they may really have belonged to Marie Antoinette.

I have never had them inspected for a signature or some other clue as to their beginnings, but if by any chance they were signed, they would be worth an absolute fortune. As it is, they are worth hundreds of times what I paid for them.

That was my first really important purchase and it was like catching a fever. From that moment on, I spent most of my free time during my travels roaming through antique shops and talking to the dealers. I learned so much from antique dealers, and they spent time with me, teaching me everything they knew about antiques. After all, I was a pretty, young star who had their undivided attention. They liked that and I took advantage of it. The only place I couldn't find antique shops in the 1950s was in Las Vegas. But today, they have everything in the world there, including antique shops.

There was a little old man in Boston named Mr. Levin. He was quite ancient, and had lots to teach me about antiques. In Houston, there were two ladies with a shop called The Green Bottle. I learned a lot from them about American furniture and clocks. They actually owned one whole street in Houston, and each house was filled with treasures. The women had been buying and stockpiling for years. Very few people were buying antiques in the 1950s and you could get marvelous things for practically nothing.

My house on Central Avenue was my creative outlet. Not only did I restore it by having it completely rewired and all new pipes put in, but I moved walls, put in central air, pushed the front entrance out eight feet and a few other things, which the contractor told me couldn't be done. After that came the yard, which also needed a complete makeover. Then, I decorated and fixed and filled the place with beautiful things.

I loved all of my beautiful things. When I look at a painting or a piece of porcelain, I see the beauty of it first. But then I see the workmanship, the hours of labor and the dedication of the artist.

Because I was such a perfectionist in my own art and the object of my craft was to make something beautiful, my possessions became like a physical manifestation of my own thoughts. I wanted to surround myself with pearls of beauty.

One of my special spots on the property was a wonderful little Japanese "tea house" built in the back yard, with furniture and running water. Eventually, I made that whole side of the house into a little oriental garden and patio.

The Music Room, which was an appendage to the house, was painted a different color than the rest of the exterior. My friend and decorator, Roy Monday, designed it all. He painted it a pale gray and the molding around the roof in black. Then there was a Chinese red stripe just below the trim to give it the oriental feeling. On the property line, across the brick patio from the Music Room door, we put up a fence made of bamboo.

At one end of the patio was a large oriental statue and at the other end, next to the teahouse, was a little stream bed laid out in white rocks, with water coming out of a hidden faucet in a large black volcanic rock. It was surrounded by greenery and in the spring, lots of blue iris would bloom.

My friend, Robert Prest, had built the little house as a playhouse for my children before we turned it into a Japanese teahouse. We took down the end wall and built an open porch off of it with a thick wood beam extending from the roof, which we covered with carved oriental motifs and painted black. It already had electricity and running water and we made it a place to barbeque right over the little pretend stream.

George Touliatos, our Theatre Memphis stage director, was given the job of lighting the teahouse. He wanted to give it the appearance of floating on water. The house was up on pilings about a foot off the ground, and underneath it were blue floodlights directed at large pieces of broken blue mirror. When the lights were on, the little house literally looked as if it was floating on water. It was an incredible effect.

At the top, we had orange spotlights giving the oriental patio an orange glow. There were no bright glaring lights, giving it a soft look. There was also a lovely deciduous holly tree that came out solid with red berries in the fall. It had the effect of a huge bouquet of red berries and it also had a somewhat oriental look.

The bamboo fencing along the property line had to be replaced every two years because it would rot and inevitably fall over. After Billy had died and I was remarried, my husband, Harry, had a big chair in the Music room next to a large window. That was where he would read the paper every morning.

Two very dear old sisters, Sophie Jameson and Eula Farnsworth, lived in the house next door by themselves and were very reclusive. They never left the confines of their property lines--ever. Someone delivered their groceries and whatever else they might need and they remained inside their house or in their backyard.

But they loved us very much. One of their greatest pleasures was watching the children playing in the yard. Once, when the fence fell down and we had to pull it out, I had to wait several weeks for the new fence that I had ordered to come in. One day, Sophie called me and said, "Marguerite, would you please not put up that bamboo fence again. We love to watch Harry in his easy chair reading the paper, and if you put that fence back up, we won't be able to see him." So, I never put it back up.

Throughout the years, I invited them over to the house several times and they never accepted. However, they were delighted for us to call on them. They always watched us in the back yard--it gave them pleasure just to know we were there.

To me, one of my greatest luxuries in life was having breakfast served in bed in my lovely home. I have a beautiful fruit wood tray with a lace-like bronze gallery around it, and elegant breakfast-sized china and silver. I also had wonderful help, who brought me my breakfast in bed.

For years, that was my time to be quiet. I never had the television on or the radio on. I didn't want any of those disturbances. I just wanted to be quiet in the morning.

When Billy was alive, we used to have breakfast in bed, side by side. It was our special time together. But once I got out of that bed and was bathed and dressed by noon, I was going 90 miles an hour and did not slow down until I got back in the bed to go to sleep, usually very late at night. Even now, I still have trouble getting up very early and going to bed early. I guess it's because I have always worked at night.

Home for the Holidays

Christmas Eve in our house was really quite something. Although I never performed on Christmas Day, I was usually performing around Christmastime. I was gone a lot when the children were little, but I always managed to get home for Christmas.

My shopping usually took place on Christmas Eve or the day before. I would go to Goldsmith's department store in Memphis and, with the help of a buyer and two huge carts; we would go up one aisle and down the other. I would point and say, "I'll have six of those, four of that, two of that, and five of this," until we filled those two carts. Then I would get bicycles and tricycles and whatever else looked like fun and take it all home where it went straight from my car to the third floor. The children were not allowed up there and it became Santa's workshop.

I had redone the attic into a lovely apartment that had a huge living room space where we dumped everything on the floor. There was an old elevator in the house and we sure appreciated it around Christmas time.

Now came the task of wrapping about a hundred presents. Nova Mae, who worked for us, would stay up all night with me and we would wrap presents. After the children went to bed, we began to bring things downstairs and Nova Mae would begin to cook while I continued wrapping presents. I stopped just before midnight to walk across the street and sing for the midnight mass. Then I would come back, and Nova Mae and I would work until six or seven in the morning.

When all the wrapping was finished, we arranged the presents so that they filled the entire front entrance hall, about 18 by 35 feet! During the months before Christmas, I used to steal away some of the children's toys and dolls, one at a time so they didn't miss them, and put them on the third floor in a room they called the "candy closet." This was just a big storage room where I kept a lot of old costumes and hats and some silver that was only used for big parties. I also kept the Easter baskets and very often bags of candy in there and I guess that's how it got its name. On Christmas Eve, we would bring down all the dolls and stuffed animals from years before and put them around the room to reappear in a big way on Christmas morning.

By daylight, I was so exhausted; I would crawl up the stairs on all fours. I could sleep for about an hour before the kids were up and that would be it. I had to be up and at 'em! No one was allowed to open anything until everyone was downstairs, and only then did the pandemonium break loose.

When the children came down, they found the front entrance hall looking like a toy store. It was absolutely covered with toys that spilled over into the living room and up the front stairs. Billy and I would sit on the steps and watch the children rip into their packages and play with all their new toys. And when they came across packages for Mama and Daddy, they would bring them over and watch as we opened them with as much curiosity as they had towards their own. What a wonderful time we had!

Easter morning in our house was another big production. We had candy in baskets and Easter bunnies and toys of all kinds. I would let the children eat all the candy they wanted for a little while and see all the little mechanical chickens that hopped and bunnies that popped out of cabbages to a musical chime. But by that evening, we'd remove most of the candy along with most of the toys. (We did the same thing at Christmas, leaving only their favorites to play with).

Everything else was put upstairs in the candy closet and brought out little by little, so that Easter and Christmas lasted a long time.

Christmas was so special to us all. I have a photograph of my son Gregory when he was about twelve years old with huge eyes filled with wonder as he surveyed his new bicycle. He just loved it, and seeing their little faces light up as they opened their presents was more exciting to me than almost anything I can think of. I think I was, and still am, as much a kid at heart as any of my six children.

Elvis

So many people ask me if I knew Elvis, with both of us celebrities living in Memphis. I didn't know him well, but I do remember singing a benefit with him for the United Way in the early stages of his career. He was so very young and really handsome. We were at opposite ends of the musical scale, and socially our lives were worlds apart. I knew he was a groundbreaking performer, but at the time of his rise to fame, I was so busy dealing with my own career and family that I never had a chance to get to know him. Looking back on it, I wish I had.

One morning in about 1969, the phone rang at 5 a.m. A man on the other end of the line said, "Marguerite Piazza?" and I managed a groggy, "Yes?"

The voice said, "This is Sam Phillips."

I said, "Hello, how are you?"

He said, "You know, I've never met you and I've been working all night and I'd like to come over to say hello and meet you."

I said, "Sam Phillips, it's 5 a.m.! I'm asleep and everybody in the house is asleep. No, I'm sorry but you can't come over right now. Call me some time later and we'll get together." So I hung up.

At 7 a.m., the phone rang again. He said, "This is Sam Phillips. I've waited long enough, so I'm coming over right now." And come over he did.

I put on a robe and went down to the music room to meet the man who had launched Elvis' career. Rebecca was awake and I asked her if she could fix some breakfast for us.

Sam had the idea to produce a current events radio talk show at 7 a.m. every morning with me as the host. However, 7 a.m. is not exactly my best time of day, so I had to refuse that one. But we talked for about an hour before he left.

Recently, I was given an Achievement Award by the University of Memphis, which they give once a year in honor of Elvis. Sam Phillips was there to present the award. When I accepted it, I told the story of Sam calling me at 5 a.m. and he said, "Yep, that's right!" But I hadn't really seen him or spoken to him since that morning until the awards dinner.

Changes

In December of 1967, I was working in Houston, Texas, where my good friend Maxine Messenger lived. That year, she gave me a tiny toy poodle puppy for Christmas, which I had been wanting for a very long time. I was so anxious to get home for the holidays that I took the late night plane from Houston to Memphis after my last show and took the little dog with me.

Maxine said she didn't think they would let me get on the plane with it, but I said, "Watch me!" I had a big fur coat on and I put a little towel in the pocket. Then I put the little puppy, just big enough to fit into the palm of my hand, into a napkin diaper, put her into my pocket and got on the airplane.

I had brought a little satchel for a dog with me, and the stewardess came over and told me that animals were not allowed on the plane. I said, "But there's nothing in there. I'm just taking it home to my dog."

Well, this was a pretty intuitive flight attendant. She just knew I had a dog somewhere, but she couldn't find it. I was praying that the little puppy wouldn't bark or make any noise, but she was very good and didn't make a peep.

I got up in the middle of the flight and went to the ladies room and put her down on some paper, and she tinkled very nicely on cue. Then I put her back in my pocket and returned to my seat. The stewardess kept coming over to me and looking around to see if she could figure out where I had that dog. But I made it home safely with Jingle Belle in my pocket.

We named her Jingle because it was Christmas, and Belle because she was a little girl. That was just four months before Billy died.

Jingle Belle is in the family portrait that year. Sadly, Billy looked so weak and so sick in that picture; in fact, he went to the hospital that night, after the pictures were taken.

After almost thirty years, my huge house began to take its toll on me. I had about twelve thousand square feet and over an acre of yard to take care of, which I wanted to be manicured to the tiniest detail. Like the girl who puts on the red shoes and dances herself to death, my dream house was killing me.

I finally gave it up because it really was taking all of my time, but I miss it. My children almost mourned the loss of the house as if it was a member of the family who had died. It was the only house the last four of them had ever known as home, and was an anchor for them when they moved out or were away.

But I have a new house now and we have new memories and experiences that make it feel like home.

My Mother's Death

While performing in Syracuse, New York, I became friends with newspaper publisher Richard Amberg and his wife, Janet. When Richard became the new editor of the Globe-Democrat in St. Louis, he called and engaged me to do another show for him in St. Louis.

When my mother was gravely ill with bone cancer in February of 1958, I found myself booked to work two weeks at the Chase Club in St. Louis. I should have cancelled it, but my mother insisted I keep my engagements. I was in St. Louis for two weeks and very upset the whole time. After the first week, I flew home on my day off. At that time, the doctors told me they had a new drug to fight the cancer, so I signed papers allowing them to give my mother nitrogen mustard, which is usually a deadly poison.

When I got back to St. Louis, Harold Koplar, who owned the Chase Hotel, was hosting a dinner in honor of his father. It was a benefit for the American Cancer Society, and he asked me if I wouldn't mind singing a few songs in between my two shows.

Of course, I agreed to do it. So I said a few words about this wonderful occasion and most worthwhile cause. I told the audience I knew about cancer firsthand because my mother was dying of cancer right then in a hospital in Memphis. I asked them to be very generous to the Cancer Society and give a little bit more for me.

I thought I was doing the right thing, but when I came off the stage, Harold came after me and almost attacked me physically. He shouted "What do you mean asking for an honor for your mother. This is a dinner in honor of my father!"

I said "Excuse me, I asked for no honor for my mother. She doesn't need any honor. She's dying. The only thing I did was to ask the people to be more generous if they could because cancer is a tragic thing to have. My mother doesn't need any honor, nor want any honor. That was not my intention."

Harold was unmoved. "Well, you can't do that. This dinner was in honor of my father and you just can't do that." He went on and on, ranting and raving.

This man was so obsessed with my supposed offense; he set about trying to sabotage my performance. He owned two hotels right next door to each other, the Chase Hotel and the Park Plaza, each with their own club. One was not used anymore, but he opened it at the last minute and sent the orchestra there for the show. He wanted me to miss the show so he could fire me!

It just so happened that, John Calli, who played the guitar, the mandolin and the banjo for me, was with the guys when they were told to go to this other show room, which had been closed for years. I couldn't believe it. But I went to the other place and did my show in an empty room, while he had people in the other hotel waiting to see me.

The next night, we never did know where we were going to be because he kept changing it back and forth. He kept saying to me, "Quit! Go home to your mother!"

And I told him "I don't quit. I'm not a quitter. I came here to do the show this week and I'm going to do it." And in spite of him, I made it through the last show, knowing that my mother was in danger of dying any minute.

One night, Richard Amberg was in the house when the second show was moved. He came back to see me and said, "Marguerite, what's going on?" So I told him about this man and what he had been doing to me.

Richard said, "If he does anything more to you, you call me and I will fix it." After the show, Mr. Koplar saw me sitting at a table with Richard Amberg and the governor of Missouri. He came up to me after they left and said, "I suppose you told Richard everything I said?"

I told him I certainly did! He stopped bothering me then, and I was at least able to play out the last few days in peace.

When I got home, I went straight to the hospital. My mother was in a horrible state. The doctors told me that the nitrogen mustard would alleviate her pain. I knew nothing about such things, so I trusted them.

That was the biggest lie I was ever told. She suffered more with that drug than with the bone cancer. It burned her alive from the inside. I was so furious with those doctors!

After a little while, my mother looked at me and said, "Marguerite, you look tired. Go home and rest. I'll see you in the morning."

I said, "Ma, I'm not that tired."

But she said, "No, I know you're tired. Go home and rest."

So, I went home and I slept. I came back early the next morning and she could no longer speak. I was terribly upset. But the doctor said to me, "Marguerite, don't you know that by this time, your mother has said everything to you that she ever wanted you to hear. Don't be upset."

I stood over her bed for almost two days, watching her endure the intense pain. When she finally died, her back was arched and her head was pulled back. No one would give her water for fear she would choke.

I'd ask her, "Ma, you want some water?" And she indicated, "Yes." So I took a straw and got a couple of drops in it and she would stick her tongue out so I could put two drops of water on it. That was the last thing I could really do for her.

When she died, Billy sent my Aunt Ann and me out into the hall to go do something. He could see that death was imminent and he didn't want me to be there. He stayed and held her hand while she died. I'll always be grateful for that.

My mother had asked me to put her makeup on when she died. I should have done it right then, but I just couldn't. They wrapped her face so it would set properly and I did it later, but she was already cold and it was very difficult.

That day and for several months after my mother's death, I couldn't cry. An odd feeling came over me. I felt an enormous responsibility to hold myself together while I arranged her funeral, rode the train which would take her body back to New Orleans, attend the services and deal with my family there. It wasn't until I found myself on a plane coming home from London, where I had sung at the Palladium, that I looked out my window. There, in the clouds, I saw my mother and the intense grief I had tried to suppress, surfaced all at once. I finally broke down and cried almost all the way home.

My Perfect Bubble Bursts

More changes were in store for me. My life with Billy Condon was absolutely wonderful until the day some dear soul had to go and tell me he was having an affair. That was the worst day of my life.

Of all the things I've had to endure, finding out about Billy's infidelity was the only time in my life that the thought of suicide ever even crossed my mind. But then, I thought about the children and I said to myself, "How could I do that? No, I couldn't do that. They need me."

So, I got rid of that thought and replaced it with, "I'll take care of that girl and I'll get him back," which is exactly what I did. I loved Billy Condon and I believed he was worth having. Billy was so very attractive and so sweet to everybody that women just wouldn't leave him alone.

Not long after I found out, I was invited to a luncheon honoring the ten best-dressed women in Memphis, of which I was one. I was dressed to the hilt in a fabulous suit, carrying Grandfather Condon's thin, delicate, gold-headed cane. As I drove out of the University Club parking lot, I had a funny feeling that I knew where Billy was.

I drove to his friend, Walter West's, apartment. It was about three in the afternoon and I parked my car, willed myself up the stairs, and knocked on the door. Billy opened it and there they were, together, in swimsuits. I walked in, dressed like a queen and said to that girl "I want to tell you something. You had best get yourself out of here. Just go on home, wherever it is."

Then I said, "Billy Condon, I'm leaving here and I want you home in fifteen minutes!" Then I turned and walked out.

Billy got home fast, but now he had to face the music with me. I knew I did not want to lose my husband. I could have done all sorts of things, like say, "I'll sue you for divorce," but I didn't want that. I wanted him and I wanted that girl gone.

So I talked to him and told him, "You can't have that. You've got us. We're your family and that's the way it is." He was very upset that I'd found out about his escapade, and that I'd confronted him with it in such a straightforward way.

That night, he became even more upset, so much so that it frightened me. He was ranting and raving. At midnight, I picked up the phone and called Monsignor Kearney at the rectory across the street and said, "Monsignor, I think you have to come over here and talk to Billy right now."

He said, "What's the matter?"

I said, "Just come, please." Monsignor threw on his clothes and came running across the street.

Monsignor Kearney really read the riot act to Billy, who was so upset he didn't know what to do with his emotions. He couldn't stand being confronted with something that he didn't want to face. He knew he'd done something wrong and he did want it to be over, he just didn't know how to get there. In all the time I'd known him, I had never seen him that upset.

When Monsignor finally left, Billy had calmed down enough that at least he wasn't going anywhere. We had nothing to do with each other for about two months. It took him that long to get over it. But he finally did, and that's when I had my fifth child, Marguerite.

Monsignor Kearney

Monsignor Kearney, who came to my rescue with Billy that fateful night, was not only a good friend, but a great part of my life. The church and the rectory were right across the street from my house and Monsignor was always coming over. He would just walk in unannounced to say hello.

He always had some sort of joke to play on the kids. Once, he came over and with a very serious look on his face, he pointed his index finger and pressed it into the shoulder of my son and said, "Billy boy, I've only got one thing against you!"

My son looked up at him wide eyed, and Monsignor said, "My finger!" and all the kids would break up laughing. Other times, he would have some squeaky toy up the big sleeves of his robes and he insisted that it was a little bird that lived up there. He used to play a funny song on the piano about "The devil's gonna get you if you don't watch out." He was just lots of fun, and the children all loved him.

Once, he walked in the back door, sat down and started playing the piano, much to the horror of a cleaning lady who was new in the house. He also came to many of my parties, and he was always there when I needed him.

Only once did we ever have a fight, and that was over the grass in his front yard, of all things! I made a point of telling him one day that it needed to be cut. I said, "We look like the poor Catholics and all the Protestants are driving down Central Avenue saying, 'That's what the Catholics look like!'"

He got so mad at me, he said, "Why aren't you more like your mother?"

And I said, "My mother wouldn't have liked the tall grass over there either."

He stormed out of my house fuming and I didn't see him again for some weeks. But we made up. After the grass was cut!

The Monsignor's sister was a nun in Nashville, and when she died, they had the funeral mass at Immaculate Conception across the street. After the mass had started, Monsignor leaned over and asked one of the altar boys to run over to the rectory and ask his secretary, Madeline, to call Marguerite and tell her to come over right now and sing for this mass, even though the mass was already in progress!

The little boy went over to Madeline, who called me on the phone. I had been in my garden and I was filthy dirty. I said, "Madeline, I'm not dressed. I was just getting ready to take a bath. I have no makeup on and I'm a mess."

She said, "I know, Marguerite, he's crazy. Don't worry about it. You don't have to come."

I said, "Wait a minute, I'll get the music and I'll be there in a minute." So I grabbed the music and ran across the street to the church, dressed in dirty yard clothes. I went straight upstairs to the choir loft and the organist couldn't believe what she was seeing. But I sang my bit and then ran out of the church so no one would see me. I went straight home and got into the tub to clean up.

After a while, the phone rang again and Monsignor said "I'm having a party in honor of my sister."

I said, "You're having a party? You just had the burial mass!"

"Yes," he said, "I'm having a lunch. Why aren't you here?"

I said, "Monsignor, I wasn't dressed. I couldn't stay."

He replied, "Do you remember that Madonna you've always wanted—the one I have in my office?"

I said, "Yes."

"If you come on over here, I'm going to give it to you."

I said, "I'll be right there." And I got over there real quick! Sure enough, after the lunch, he gave it to me and I brought it home. It's a beautiful porcelain standing Madonna painted with gold and enamels. I have bought several very nice Madonnas through the years, but the one Monsignor gave me is the one I treasure the most.

The Monsignor and I went way back. When Billy's first wife, Liz, died, I had been working in Miami and Billy was with me. Since she lived in Coral Gables, we were able to go to her funeral. After we came home, Billy said to me one day, "You know, now that Liz is gone, we can get married in the Catholic Church." We had been married for about six years by then, but since we had both been divorced, we had to be married by a justice of the peace. The Catholic faith had always been an important part of both our lives, despite the Church's disapproval of our respective divorces. When we were in Memphis, we always went to Mass on Sunday and Billy often took part by giving a reading or passing the collection basket. Now that our ex-spouses were both gone, we both wanted the Church's blessing on our marriage.

We immediately called the Monsignor and said, "How would you like to marry us in the Church?"

Without missing a beat, he replied, "I'd love to."

I called some friends who lived two blocks away and said, "Would you come over and stand up for us while we get married in the Catholic Church?"

They immediately agreed. "Oh, yes, we'd be thrilled to do it. We'll be right over."

Roy Monday, my decorator and friend, was staying with us at the time. He was living in the carriage house as our guest, so I said, "Roy, we're getting married in the church. Do you want to come across the street with us?"

"How exciting," he said. "I'd love that!"

So we all went across the street where Monsignor met us at the altar. The first thing he did was to open a little music box that played, "Deck the Halls."

I said, "Monsignor, turn that thing off. It's Christmas music."

"Oh, no," he said. "You have to have some music, and it's all I've got." So Deck the Halls was playing on the music box, and my friends, Mary Arnette and Joe Tagg, were taking their roles very seriously, complete with solemn faces. Roy was so moved by it all that he dissolved into tears.

I couldn't stop laughing at the music box and all that was going on, and Billy was laughing, too. Once Monsignor had performed the ceremony, we all went back across the street to our house. It was cocktail time, so Billy got out the champagne and said, "Rebecca, let's have some hors d'oeuvres." Monsignor joined us and we had a little party.

The kids came into the library and said, "Where were you, Mama? We couldn't find you." I told them we were across the street getting married.

"What?" little Billy asked, not understanding. He must have been about three years old.

I said, "We were getting married in the church."

"Oh," he said, and then he went off to play. It was a really funny afternoon.

Monsignor always used to tell us he was a virgin. He had become a priest, and of course had taken the vows of celibacy at a fairly young age. He was proud of the fact that he was still a virgin. Billy used to say that was quite a remarkable feat for a man of his years.

Monsignor Kearney enriched my life in many ways. He was always there for me when I had a crisis or just needed a sympathetic ear. And one of my gifts to him was to sing the midnight mass every year on Christmas Eve at the Immaculate Conception Church across the street. It wasn't until Monsignor was forced to retire and was replaced by a young priest that I stopped singing the midnight mass.

It seemed that a new bishop had come to town, making Immaculate Conception the city's cathedral. Monsignor had so wanted to be named bishop, but the church decided he was not right for the position. Now, the new bishop had come into a town that was very slow to accept change, but the Catholic community did welcome him with an elaborate ceremony in front of thousands of people at the Mid-South Coliseum.

All the clergy from the region were in attendance and, one by one, they filed onto the stage to kiss his ring and say a word of welcome. I almost went into shock as I watched Monsignor Kearney bow and kiss the ring of the new bishop, and then give him a slap across his cheek before returning to his seat. After Monsignor retired, he began to deteriorate quickly and soon after, he died. I miss him to this day.

Billy Condon's Death

About two years before Billy died, we had a fight over something I don't even remember. But in my anger I said to him, "You know, I really ought to divorce you!"

And he looked at me with a straight face and said, "Oh God, Marguerite. Can't you just wait two years?!"

I said, "What?"

And he said, "Just wait two years." He called it almost to the day. Over those two years, Billy gradually deteriorated. He would never admit he was sick. He didn't even want to go to bed at night. I think he knew he was on his way out and he decided to do everything he wanted to do, while he still had time.

That wasn't good for me or him or anybody else. But that was my opinion, not his. And he was the one who was going to die. I finally went to Rebecca and said, "Let's give him what he wants, Becky. He's a people person. He loves people, he wants to be with people, so let's just have a lot of dinner parties." And we did.

Eventually, Billy's lifestyle caught up with him. His heart began to trouble him several years before he died, but he ignored it. He abused his body by staying up half the night drinking, smoking, dancing, and carrying on.

Billy had been seeing a doctor who had repeatedly given him a clean bill of health, when Billy actually knew he was sick. One day, he decided to change doctors, and I took him to see a young internist named Dr. Walter Hoffman. After examining Billy, Dr. Hoffman insisted that he go directly to the hospital. He had an advanced heart disease and from that moment on, he became progressively worse.

I went home and packed some of his clothes and his nightshirts and brought them to the hospital. Apparently, his heart was twice the size it should have been. With rest and proper treatment, they were able to get the heart to go down. But as soon as he got out of the hospital, he began living just like he had before, smoking and drinking and not getting enough rest. Billy was not an offensive drinker. He didn't smoke or drink during the day. But at five o'clock, he became a "social drinker and smoker."

After that first stay in the hospital, he was in and out of hospitals for the rest of his life. When he was home for a while, we had to give him oxygen, and there was always a big tank next to the bed. He never complained because he didn't want anyone to know that he was sick, but I could see the suffering in his eyes.

When Dr. Hoffman put him in the hospital a second time, he got up one morning at about six, dressed himself and went downstairs without permission. One of the nurses saw him and said, "Mr. Condon, you can't leave."

But he kept walking and said, "I'll be right back." He opened the heavy glass door, got into a taxi and said, "Take me home."

I have always been a very light sleeper and when I heard someone downstairs at 6:30 in the morning, I got up to see who it was. I crept to the top of the back stairs, knowing Billy was in the hospital. When I saw that familiar green felt hat of his sail from the kitchen into the back hall, I thought, *That can't be Billy. It just can't!*

I ran downstairs and found him in the library pouring himself a martini. I couldn't believe my eyes. I said, "Billy, what are you doing?"

He just looked at me and said, "I just had to have a drink."

I was beside myself with worry. "Billy, you're not supposed to be out of the hospital!"

But he said, "Don't worry, I have a taxi waiting. He's gonna take me back." So he drank his martini and got back in the taxi. I ran out after him in my nightgown and robe to ask the taxi driver to please get out and open the hospital door for him, and he promised me he would do that. So Billy went back to the hospital, where he stayed. He just had to have a drink.

Before Billy went into the hospital for the last time, he had good days and bad days. As I have said, he never wanted to admit he was sick and his sense of humor prevailed, despite all his suffering. When he was still able to, he would put on a pair of trousers with a beautiful silk paisley robe and an ascot tied around his neck and come downstairs to receive visitors. He made light of his very serious illness by telling jokes and making everyone laugh.

One of his favorite stories had to do with terrorizing a nurse. He would tell how he had sneaked a flask of scotch into the hospital in the pocket of his robe and kept it hidden in his nightstand. One morning, an unsuspecting nurse brought him a small cup and asked for a urine specimen. Then she left the room, promising to be back in a few minutes. That was when Billy got the bright idea to pour scotch into the cup. When the nurse returned, she commented that the urine sample looked rather dark. At that, Billy said, "Well, let's run it through one more time!" and swallowed the shot of whiskey in a single gulp.

When we took him back to the hospital for the last time, I knew he was very seriously ill. I asked the people taking care of him to let him die when it was his time to go, and not to try to preserve him for another day or another hour, because it would be too hard on him.

But they did not honor my request. I was with him in his room one day when suddenly his face became a mask of tragedy. His mouth went down on the sides and it was as if he were frozen in time.

I hadn't expected it to be like that and I didn't know what to do. Billy seemed to have stopped breathing. I looked at him and instinct took over. I said, "Hold on, Billy! Hold on!"

I ran out into the hallway, but the nurse was not there, so I ran until I found another nurse. I screamed, "Come quick!" The alarm was sounded and a team of doctors came running in.

Billy was technically dead when they got there, and they threw me out of the room as the doctors came down the hall with all their machines. They cut his pajamas off of him and they actually brought him back to life. They put all kinds of tubes and wires in and around him to monitor everything. Then, instead of letting him go peacefully, the doctors kept him alive for three horrible days, during which he suffered the tortures of the damned.

There was nothing these doctors could have done for him at that point. There was no cure, no help. Billy Condon had experienced heart failure. Both sides of his heart were affected, and when the heart quits functioning, the kidneys also begin to deteriorate.

When it came to his ultimate illness, what Billy needed was a heart transplant. But such procedures had not been developed yet. I remember asking him once what he wanted for his birthday. His reply was, "A new heart. What I need is a new heart."

Coincidentally, we actually knew Dr. Denton Cooley, who did one of the first heart transplants. As a matter of fact, Billy and Denton were dead ringers for one another. Once, when Denton Cooley operated on my friend, Maxine Messenger, she came out of the anesthesia, looked up at Denton standing over her and said, "Oh, Billy, how are you?" I also knew Dr. DeBakey, the first man to perform a heart transplant. But there was nothing they could have done for Billy back in those days.

Now, still technically alive, Billy was put in intensive care, where he swelled up like a frog. When the nurses turned him on his side, one side would go down. But when they turned him again, the other side would swell. He was almost unidentifiable as the man who once had been. My worst fears were being realized.

Billy suffered terribly, and for what reason? One day, they let me go in and see him. He couldn't speak, but when he realized it was me, he mustered all the strength he had for the enormous effort of saying to me, "Let's go home."

I said, "We'll go home, Billy. I promise you, we'll go home." I was so upset I couldn't talk to him. So I sang Danny Boy to him and it soothed him. Then, the nurses made me leave. He died shortly after that.

Afterwards, when we had him laid out, the swelling had gone down and he looked like himself. His eyes were a little open at first. He had the most beautiful big gray eyes. I closed them for the last time.

His funeral was quite wonderful. A musician friend of mine, Joe D'Gerolimo, who played the trumpet, played a sort of announcement of eternity and was joined by several other musicians. The church was overflowing as several hundred people had come to pay their respects. Billy was certainly loved by many, many people. But none more than me. He was truly the great love of my life. And here I was again, lost in the tumultuous wake that men always seemed to leave in my life. But the devastation of my loss would soon be replaced by a fight for my own life.

170

Camel Ad 1957

Norell Dress for Third Act

Party at Memphis Hunt and Polo Club 1961

Christmas Card 1961

Part Six

Cancer: The First Signs

The year was 1960, and for weeks I had been bothered by a small pink spot on my right cheek. I kept expecting it to go away, but it was still there. I was getting ready for my opening at the Persian Room of the Plaza Hotel in New York City and I really wanted to look perfect that night because I knew several important critics would be there.

I've always been overly conscious about my looks. I've been known to drive hairdressers crazy if every hair wasn't just the way I wanted it. But there was nothing I could do about that pink spot. So I just put on two extra coats of makeup and hoped no one would notice.

I had been working eleven months out of the year in those days, and I had very little time at home with my husband and four children. I never bothered to take time out to see a doctor.

Four years later, in 1964, when I was playing the Roosevelt Hotel in New Orleans and the lights on my little table for the Pagliacci routine came down on my nose, I asked the doctor who sewed me up if he would take a look at the spot on my face.

"Oh", he said, "I know you think it's skin cancer. But it's nothing. Forget it."

A year later, I noticed it was starting to spread. So I went to a dermatologist in Memphis, who took a little piece for analysis. His report sent a chill through me. It was cancerous. I had already seen first-hand what cancer could do. I watched my mother lose her terribly painful two-year battle with the disease in 1958. And I was shattered by the diagnosis.

"If you were just an ordinary person," the doctor said, "I would simply burn it off or cut it out. But since your face is so important to your career, I think you should have a plastic surgeon do it." So I found a plastic surgeon in Memphis and arranged for the operation.

I always had great rapport with the press. They were very good to me and I appreciated it and treated them with respect in return. But one columnist in particular became one of my best friends and an important person in my life. Her name was Maxine Messinger.

When I had the first operation for the cancer on my face in the early 1960s, before we knew what it was, Maxine came to Memphis to be with me. Still wavering in and out of the anesthesia, I was wheeled back into my hospital room. When the phone rang, Maxine was there to pick it up. It was the editor of the Houston Chronicle.

He told her, "I have good news and I have bad news." The bad news was that her paper, The Post, had folded and everyone was out of work.

"Oh" she said. "That's terrible."

I kept mumbling, "What is it, Maxine?"

She told me, "The Post closed. It's in bankruptcy."

Then he said, "The good news is I am going to hire two people from the Post and give them jobs at the Chronicle and one of them is you. Can you come home immediately?"

She said, "That's very nice of you, but I can't come home right now. I'm with a friend, Marguerite Piazza, and she's just had an operation. I can't leave her right now."

"Can you be here in two days?" he asked. Yes, she could do that. And that's how she got the job with the Houston Chronicle. But trying to talk to that man about her future and dealing with me in my still drugged state was traumatic for her. She was very flustered.

When she hung up the phone she said, "Oh, my God, I just told that man who was kind enough to give me a job that I couldn't be there for two days. I can't believe I said that."

Maxine later developed multiple sclerosis, which she lived with secretly for a very long time. I knew the pain she was in long before it became public knowledge. She was afraid she would lose her job, her life's work and enjoyment if the paper ever found out. But they so loved Maxine that when her insurance ran out, they bought another policy for a million dollars.

With that, she gathered all her doctors in a room and told them this money was to pay for their services, and when it ran out, she expected them to keep on treating her. They all laughed, but said yes, they would.

I was not as brave a soul as Maxine when it came to facing hospitalization. In fact, the thought of any surgery, even minor surgery, was terrifying to me. I had never had an operation before and my only trips to the hospital had been to have my children.

I checked into the hospital the night before the surgery and spent a very restless night. As it turned out, it wasn't such a simple operation after all. It took three and a half hours. But the pathologist gave a verdict of "simple skin cancer" rather than melanoma and nobody expected to hear any more about it.

I was elated. Except for the tiny scar on my right cheek, which I was able to cover with makeup, I was back in business. In fact, I was back singing within a few weeks.

A year later, I went back to see the doctor. The spot was still quite pink, so he photographed it and told me it just had not healed.

I ignored it for another two years, simply covering it with makeup. But ignoring cancer is the worst thing you can do. If you don't heed the warning signals and solve the problem early, a time may come when it's too late. Like most things in life, timing is everything.

About this time, my husband Billy began to get sick. Even while he was so ill and in so much pain, he kept telling me that I should go see somebody else about that spot on my face. But I was much too busy with my chaotic life to take his advice.

After Billy died, I realized I was the only one the children had left, so I decided to do what I had put off doing for so long. I went to another doctor, and this time the pathologist said it was melanoma, the type of cancer most likely to spread and one of the most deadly forms. I was stunned.

On top of that, he felt I needed another operation; this time, we would remove the glands to prevent it from spreading. To confirm his diagnosis, I went to see another pathologist in St. Louis, who studied all the slides from the earlier biopsies and decided that after removing the spot, no further surgery would be needed.

He told me that my glands had not been affected, calling my spot a "melanotic freckle." But he did warn me that if it returned, it would return along the line of the incision.

Traveling in Europe

Relieved by this last diagnosis, I took three of my children and went to Europe for the summer. I had performed at the Press Club in Washington D.C. when the mayor of Florence, Italy came over to

175

thank the American people for helping save Florence after a terrible flood.

Alitalia Airlines sponsored the event and asked me to perform, which I did without pay. As an unexpected gift, Alitalia gave me four first-class tickets to use at my discretion, wherever I wanted to go.

I decided to take three of my children, Jimmy, who was 15, Shirley, 13, and Billy, 10. The two little girls, Anna-Becky and Marguerite, were too young, so they stayed home with Becky. My oldest child, Gregory, was already over there. He was now eighteen years old and in the army. His number to be drafted was very high, so he had enlisted and, an accomplished drummer, got into the army band.

Gregory was stationed in Frankfurt, Germany, and I thought I would surprise him by arriving with three of his sisters and brothers for a visit at his army camp. My friend, Fred Goldsmith, whom I had been dating, helped me prepare for this trip. He saw to my itinerary and took care of many of the details. We decided at the last minute that I'd better let Gregory know we were coming.

I sent a wire to the army base in Frankfurt and didn't hear anything back for days. Then I decided to call to try locating him. I didn't want to get over there and miss him. When I called the army base, I was told that the band was taking a month's vacation and everybody had left the base.

Since I had the tickets and we were all packed and ready to go the next morning, I decided we would just go. That night I recorded a new song at one of the recording studios in Memphis. I have no idea what happened to that recording. My life became so upset after that, I simply forgot about it.

Before I went to bed that night, I called Fred Goldsmith and said, "Please keep in contact with Rebecca, the children's nurse. If Gregory should call home, I want to find out where he is."

Then I hung up and said a little prayer. I said, "God, if you could just let Gregory have a little bitty wreck... not a big wreck, I don't want him to get hurt or anything, just damage the car so he'll have to call home for money. Would you please just do that for me Lord? I need to find this boy."

Our first stop was Portugal, which was lovely. We spent two days and had a great time. Not long after we arrived, I received an urgent message to call Fred Goldsmith in Memphis, Tennessee.

When he heard my voice, he said, "You're not going to believe this, but Gregory had a little wreck and he needed $600 to fix his car. He's in London and he's just fine." He told me not to worry, he'd already sent the money and Gregory should get it that day.

I said, "Thank you so much Fred. I'll reimburse you when I get back." But now I had Gregory's number, and I called him in London to say, "Get yourself back to Frankfurt. We're on our way." He did just that and when we finally arrived, there was Gregory to meet us. It was a miracle!

What a wonderful time we had in Frankfurt! We saw everything there was to see and then went shopping. I bought a gorgeous fur bedspread for Gregory, which he was crazy about. I also bought him a brand new, four-door BMW. It was so inexpensive, I could hardly believe it. He drove it all over Europe and then brought it home with him as a used car.

After Germany, we went to Venice. A gondola took us to our hotel, and the children thought we were in a fairy tale city. When we got to our rooms, we found ourselves on the second floor. I opened the shutters and there below the window was a gondolier singing away.

The children started to nudge me and say, "Mama, sing something! Sing out the window to them."

I said, "Don't be ridiculous, I can't do that."

"Oh, yes you can," they said. "Come on, come on. Do it. Sing something!"

Well, they wouldn't let me out of it, so when he ended his song, I started to sing "O Sole Mio." A little crowd gathered below my window and when I finished, they all cheered. At that point, we all felt as if we were in a movie. We had a great time in Venice.

Our next stop was Paris and then it was almost time to go home. But my son, Jimmy, decided he wanted to stay in Europe. There was only one problem. He didn't have any money and I thought a fifteen-year-old was too young to be roaming around Europe by himself.

However, Jimmy knew just what buttons to push on his Italian Mama. He went on a hunger strike in his hotel room in Paris and refused to eat or drink anything. In two days, he had a high fever and wouldn't get out of bed. We were locked in a battle of wills until I realized the level of his determination. He was going to kill himself.

I had to give in. I gave him a hundred dollars and his ticket and said, "When the hundred dollars runs out, come home." In those days, you really could stay in youth hostels and do it for almost no money.

But what did he do? He took himself back to Spain, where he found a Spanish family to live with. For a dollar a day, he had a place to sleep and two meals. He picked up the language in no time and spent almost every day in the museums.

Jimmy was an artist and had the mind of an irrational genius. After Spain, he went to London and lived with another family for a dollar a day. He also bought himself some very expensive shirts. Finally, when the money ran out, he came home.

My daughter, Shirley, who was in her unmanageable teens, also gave me a hard time. Nothing seemed to please her and she wanted to go home. When we were in Rome, we walked by the Spanish Steps, and some of the men tried to pinch Shirley's rear end, which was the custom in those days.

I heard one of them say in Italian "Watch out for the duena," meaning the old lady. Were they talking about me? I thought to myself, the last time I was here it was *my* rear end they were pinching!

Only one child was my comfort and joy on that trip: Billy, then about ten years old. One day in Paris when I was trying to change Jimmy's tickets, it was about 100 degrees outside and there was no air conditioning in the place. I thought I was going to have a stroke.

Billy left and went into the perfume shop next door. He returned with a present for me. He said, "Mama, I bought you a lovely bottle of perfume. Now, I don't want you to be upset anymore."

And to think I almost didn't bring him because I thought he was too young and might make trouble. He was the only one who didn't!

After Jimmy took off on his adventure, I sent the other two children home as I had planned to do, and met my friend Arthur Spitzer in Rome. We went to a great restaurant called "O Mia Petaca," where all the waiters sang and there were mimes to entertain us.

The next day, we flew to Greece, where Arthur had rented a yacht. There were seven of us altogether, including Jack Warner's two daughters. One had been married to King Vidor, the famous American movie director, but he had died, and she was quite unhappy.

178

In addition to the guests, there were seven or eight crew on this beautiful ship. We had an excellent chef who created everything from French cuisine to Greek delicacies.

After a few days out, the seas became really rough, which made me very nervous. Every time we pulled into port, I would threaten to go home. But Arthur said, "No you're not, you're staying."

One night, it was very rough, even in port. We were anchored at one of the islands and everybody said they were going to a hotel. I declined, saying I wasn't going to a hotel with Arthur because it wouldn't look right. I would stay on board. So off I went to bed. The only other person on board was Mrs. Vidor, who had so many pills in her that I don't think she knew if she was on a boat or on the moon.

I barely closed my eyes all night. The next morning it was still rough. At breakfast, I almost couldn't take it any more, and I broke down and cried. Then, I got up and left the breakfast table.

The last day on the yacht with my friends, I got up early. When I looked at myself in the mirror, I saw it. There was a pink rash along the line of the scar on my face. That was what the doctors told me to watch for, because if that happened, it would mean the cancer was back. The old fear gripped my insides again, but I remained outwardly calm. I decided to put it out of my mind until I could do something about it.

My Second Cancer Surgery

As soon as I got home, I went right to the doctor's office and he said, "That's it. We'll have to operate again." I asked him if it could wait until Monday so I could perform a job in Atlanta. I sang on Saturday night, then returned to Memphis for my third operation.

Once again, the pathologist said it was melanoma. The plastic surgeon recommended a cancer specialist in Memphis, who said there was no longer any use trying to save my face; I would have to have radical surgery. This meant I was to lose my right cheek, as well as a large piece of skin from my neck to cover my face. All thought of career and beauty flew out the window. I was now in a struggle for my life.

My own family, my two aunts in New Orleans, and my late husband Billy's brother and sister-in-law decided simultaneously that I should seek the best the world had to offer. They insisted I go to

Memorial Sloan-Kettering in New York and consult a head and neck cancer specialist. It was now early October, 1968.

Two days later, I was in New York, where I met the man who was to save my life. Dr. Edgar Frizell, the head of the Department of Head and Neck Surgery, explained the radical operation to me. He admitted he would have to "mutilate" me, but he added that it was "better to be scarred up and alive than to be a beautiful corpse!" There was not much of a decision to be made.

Dr. Frizell agreed to do the surgery, but since only a week had passed since my last operation, he felt I should go home and let that heal for another week. I had been home only four days when I got an urgent call from him. He said, "Come back immediately. We feel sure it has spread to the glands."

Until this time, I had truly been calm. Even after I received the doctor's phone call, I kept a dinner date at a friend's house. But just before dinner was served, a strange feeling came over me. All I knew was that I had to get out of that house... fast.

I stood up from the dinner table, walked out and drove the two blocks home by myself. When I walked in the back door, I went completely to pieces. It was nine o'clock and my Aunt Ann, who had come up from her home in Thibodeaux, Louisiana, was alone in the house. The children were out to dinner with Becky.

I became hysterical and it took all of Ann's strength to get me into bed. It seemed the world was falling to pieces around me and I just lost all control of my life.

The children got home about an hour and a half later and were wonderful. They all climbed onto the bed, surrounded me and held my hands and kissed me. Even the baby, Anna-Becky, then six years old, kept saying, "Mama, it's all right."

My aunt phoned the doctor, who sent over a tranquilizer, but I refused to take it. The hysteria continued until midnight and the children didn't leave me for a second. Finally, I came out of it and fell asleep from utter exhaustion. I have never broken down again since that day. In fact, a strange calm came over me and stayed, even during that session in New York when I learned how much of my face I was to lose.

I returned to New York the next day, ready to enter Memorial Hospital. My Aunt Ann came with me and my manager, Raymond Katz, flew in from the West Coast.

A good friend from Houston, John W. Mecom, Sr., was in town on business and asked me what I wanted to do that night before entering the hospital. Because Peggy Lee was playing at the Copacabana, I decided I'd like to be in the friendly surroundings of a nightclub. I even considered that it might well be my last time in a nightclub, or anywhere else for that matter. So we went to the Copa's midnight show and it was the wee hours of the morning when we got home.

As I look back on that evening, I am amazed that I was actually able to concentrate on Peggy Lee's show and to enjoy watching such a fine performer at work. Every once in awhile though, I caught myself wondering if I would ever be in the spotlight again.

After my night out, I spent the afternoon in the cold, antiseptic bowels of New York's Memorial Sloan-Kettering Hospital, surrounded by other skin cancer patients who were more or less in the same boat. It interested me that they were all so surprisingly calm, even rather detached.

The doctor came looking for me in the Radiology Department with a plastic surgeon at his heels. I had wanted my plastic surgeon and dear friend, Macarthy Demere from Memphis, to come to New York and do the closure for my cancer surgery. I thought if Mac was to close the wound, it would be less horrible. But Dr. Frizell refused my request. He told me that he knew what he had to do to save my life, and he didn't want anyone standing over him while he was doing it. Besides, he said, there was a plastic surgeon here in New York who worked with him.

I was taken into a consultation room where the plastic surgeon began to advise Dr. Frizell about the incision and what he should do with the flap of skin he was to take from my neck to put over where he would remove my cheek. It was during this session that I found out the plastic surgeon had his day off the following day, the day they had scheduled my surgery.

Now, he gingerly pulled a tissue from the box on the table and held it from behind my ear to the front of my neck. Then he stretched it from under my ear across my face, all the way to my nose and said, "I think this will do. After you remove the cancer, cut about this much skin, then pull it up under the ear and onto the cheek and sew it in."

Even through my fear and misery, I couldn't help comparing it to cutting and sewing a piece of fabric. I lamely joked, "Hey, you'd better get another quarter of an inch. God forbid you should be short." But they were not amused.

In fact, I was very close to the edge. My husband had just died seven months earlier and I really had no one close to advise me or console me. I was on my own and I knew that I had six children at home who would become orphans if this cancer, this threat to my life, succeeded or if this doctor failed. Joking was my way of coping.

During my consultation, I was told about another possible consequence of the operation. In radical surgery, there is always the issue of the facial nerve. The doctor warned me that he might not be able to save it. This would mean I could have complete paralysis on the right side of my face, and that my speech would be affected. I put myself in God's hands that night as I went to sleep.

Early the next morning, they knocked me out with a shot and I knew nothing again until late that night. The operation took five hours and I was in the recovery room for ten hours. When I came out of the haze of drugs, my Aunt Ann and the doctor were leaning over me and Ann was saying bravely, "Oh, you're just fine, Marguerite. It's not bad at all." What I didn't know was that when they first wheeled me into the room she had flown out into the hall and become hysterical.

The doctor suggested that all the mirrors in the room be covered. He thought it would be better if I couldn't look at myself for the first few days. I knew that I wouldn't be able to bear it. From everything I've heard since, I must have been a horrible sight.

I was enormously swollen, terribly bruised, and scarred. My face was a patchwork of ugly black stitches. Even though the doctor had miraculously been able to save my facial nerve, there was some temporary damage. The right side of my face was paralyzed. I didn't know it, but my right eye did not close when I blinked. Fortunately, most of that vanished within about two weeks.

The skin flap on my cheek was bright purple, which alarmed the doctors, and there was some doubt whether the skin that had been grafted would take. Again, God was on my side and the flap took.

The operation was performed on a Wednesday morning, and it seemed like an eternity until the following Monday, when I got the pathologist's report. During that time, Kate Smith, the great singer who was famous for introducing the song "God Bless America," had come to visit me in the hospital and brought me a bottle of champagne.

About nine o'clock Monday evening, Aunt Ann and I were in the room when a young resident came in. He said, "The report has just come back and I know I shouldn't do this. I should wait until tomorrow morning and let Dr. Frizell tell you. But I know you want to know. There was no cancer in your glands. The report says you're clear."

I said, "Bravo! Get that bottle of champagne Kate Smith brought here and let's have a little toast." It was great news. It meant life. At the time, I was so thrilled to be given a clean report that I never thought to complain about the procedure. I felt as though I had been freed from something horrible, which indeed, I had.

But looking back on the whole ordeal, I wonder why there wasn't some sort of exploratory surgery, a biopsy perhaps, to see if the glands were really affected before removing them and a good portion of my neck, as well as the entire muscle from the front of my right shoulder.

As it turned out, the cancer had not spread to the lymph glands. I probably would not be here today if it had. But the doctors had butchered me as if it had.

They cut the nerve and removed the muscle in my right shoulder so they could get at my lymph glands to remove them. I still don't have full use of my right arm and I was not informed that they were going to do that. It was yet another surprise after the surgery.

In fact, I later learned that the procedure they performed on me in New York was an old one which was discontinued less than a year after I had my surgery. I believe now that if I'd had the surgery in Memphis, I would be a lot less scarred. They were already ahead of New York in this field of medicine, and may not have taken such drastic measures.

Throughout my crises, I have relied heavily on my family and a few dear friends for support. My family especially has always been there for me; through four marriages, six children, a full time career on the road and then, with my fight for survival against cancer.

After my radical surgery, I was in Sloane Kettering for two weeks, during which a few of my closest friends came to see me. Marion and Teddy Donahue came over one day and asked if I would like to go for a ride in the car. It was a beautiful afternoon and I thought it sounded great to get out of the hospital for a few minutes.

Of course, I couldn't get out of the car. I didn't have the energy and I was a sight to look at. The chauffeur brought their car around to the front door, and with a big coat over my pajamas and a pair of shoes, I did take a short ride.

I wasn't gone very long before they brought me back and I got in the bed again. But because I had left for that brief time, my insurance would not pay for that day in the hospital. I didn't care. That one little outing did so much for me psychologically that it probably saved the insurance company an extra week of hospital stay.

About eight or nine months after the radical surgery in New York, I began a series of operations to correct all the things that were done that day, which were horrendous. Some of them were big and some of them were smaller procedures.

Recovery

I had been left with a lot of scar tissue after my surgery, and my neck was lined with a thick, hard band of it. It felt as if I were wearing a heavy-duty rubber band around my neck all the time. My doctor in Memphis, Dr. Mac Demere, had to go in and clip that scar tissue at various points to release my neck and make it move more freely.

I still feel slightly bound on the right side of my neck, which is still not free like the other side, but is much freer now than it was then. We worked slowly, one operation at a time, to carve out the scarring on my face where Dr. Frizell had sewn in the skin from my neck.

Unfortunately, my body produces excessive keloids, which cause scarring, and whenever anyone cuts me they have to be very careful.

After each of those operations, and there were many, I was not allowed to speak for a week to ten days. I remember Rebecca asking me what she could do, as I was frequently going in for surgery. I always asked her to please have a pot of soup made when I got home from the hospital. And she always did.

It's a good thing I'm a soup freak. Even today, I have some sort of soup almost every day for lunch. In fact, I always had a big pot of soup on the stove, which contained chunks of beef or chicken and lots of vegetables. She would then put it in the blender until it was completely pureed so I could drink it without moving my stitches. Even the simplest act of eating took time and dedication.

Barely four months after the radical surgery, I made my first public appearance singing "The Star Spangled Banner" at the first Inaugural Gala for President Nixon in January 1969. I opened the show and I'll never forget it. I was escorted on stage by two Marines, one black and one white. They were both gorgeous young men, tall, well-built, and beautifully uniformed. They stood, one on each side of me while I sang, then escorted me down.

It was a great experience for me to know that even with the patch on my face and the scars, people still wanted me to sing. And I will always be grateful to Richard Nixon for asking me to do that. I had to cancel quite a few jobs for the operation and during my recovery. But with my newfound confidence from that single performance, I was soon back on stage.

Six weeks after the inaugural, I was asked to do a benefit at the Shamrock Hilton in Houston. Until that time, I didn't have the courage to perform my entire act in a supper club. I didn't know whether I had the strength or whether my voice would hold out for the fifty minutes I had to be on stage. But I decided it would be as good a time as any to test my wings and my voice.

I spent the entire day of the engagement rehearsing with the orchestra. The rehearsal went well enough, even though I held my voice back for fear I would exhaust it before show time. I also spent a long time with the lighting technician. I had a close friend come to the rehearsal and sit all around the room to check the visibility of my scars as we set the lights. He assured me it was next to impossible to detect them, but I really didn't believe him.

As show time approached, I felt my nerves taking over. I sat upstairs in my suite going over and over the lyrics of my songs. Though it had only been about six months, it felt like ages since I had performed an entire show and I was sure I wouldn't remember a word. I fussed an unusually long time with my makeup, unable to bear people seeing my scars and feeling sorry for me, rather than enjoying the show. I didn't want people to applaud out of pity. I wanted to be good at what I did and to be appreciated for that, not because I'd survived an operation.

I feel the same way about my age. I don't tell people how old I am because I don't want it to be an issue. I don't want people to say, "She's great for a ____ year old." To this day, when I get up onstage in front of an audience, I undergo a transformation. I feel and sing and move as I did twenty or thirty years ago.

But no matter what I did that night in Houston, I felt there was no way to hide the scars. In my mind, they were magnified tenfold. I knew that I could sing, but I didn't know how the audience would accept me.

Just as I got to my offstage dressing room to re-check my makeup, I heard the music. Then the bandleader was saying, "Here she is, the star of stage, television, the Metropolitan Opera and the star of our show, the lovely Miss Marguerite Piazza."

I didn't feel at all like a star at that moment, nor did I feel especially lovely. I had butterflies in my stomach, my heart was pounding, and my hands were shaking as I walked onto the stage.

There was a warm, friendly audience applauding me and welcoming me back before I ever started to sing and it felt wonderful. Mechanically, I started to sing my first number, and the years of experience in the spotlight came rushing back.

It took the first number for me to get my feet firmly planted on the stage. My voice was behaving beautifully and I knew the audience was giving me their full attention. By the end of the second number, I was beginning to enjoy myself. Before I knew it, I was performing as if nothing had ever happened. I could feel all the old confidence come back.

That was the first time I felt I was winning my fight with cancer. You know, it's amazing, if I hadn't had my career all through the trials and tribulations I've had in my life, I doubt that I would still be here.

Giving a performance is very demanding work. And being the perfectionist that I am only made it more so. When I am performing, I cannot think of anything else. Nothing is allowed to enter my mind except the interpretation of the songs that I'm singing. It requires a total release from every worry that I might be having at the time, no matter how serious.

Performing is about controlling and directing my mind to do what I wanted it to do and to make my body follow suit. I seemed to come by this ability naturally and I used it regularly. But I was not really aware of it consciously. If I had been aware of it earlier in life, perhaps I would have used it to change the way I did a few things, rather than just trying to survive them.

My recovery from the radical was something I had to work at constantly. After my first reappearance on a supper club stage in Houston, I took on more jobs. I went next to the Blue Room at the Roosevelt Hotel in New Orleans. I was not as nervous as I had been in Houston and became more aware of my body and my voice.

I was on the stage singing one night when I suddenly realized that I wasn't pronouncing certain letters. I couldn't sing S or F or P. Very concerned, I went to a speech therapist who gave me exercises to overcome this new development. One exercise was to try to blow out a match, which to my surprise, I couldn't do.

The other exercise involved blowing on a feather to make it move. I couldn't do that either in the beginning, but I kept doing it and doing it. The therapist also put hot packs on my face and manipulated them in a sort of facial massage. I tried to exercise my lips to form certain letters until finally the day came when I could do all those things again.

It took about eight months before I was able to speak perfectly again, and the only reason I achieved that was because of my powerful drive to get better, and to do whatever it took to achieve it.

There were several extremely annoying side effects from the radical that I was not prepared for. After my performance in New Orleans, Aunt Ann came back to Memphis with me. I kept telling myself that I had been getting better every day and I expected things to have returned to normal by this point. Ann came into my bedroom one morning as I was trying to eat a bite of breakfast.

I said, "Ann, there's something else wrong with me."

And she said, "Oh, my God, what?"

I replied, "I can't lift my arm."

She flew into a frenzy and insisted that I call the doctor in New York right then. So I did.

"Oh, that," he said, when I had presented my problem. "I had to cut out those nerves. You just won't be able to lift your arm over your head for the rest of your life."

While his bedside manner was hardly endearing, I chose to take his remarks as a challenge. After I hung up the phone, I used my back muscle and found that if I brought my arm forward, I could lift it above my head.

I was so pleased with myself that I practiced this every day. I stood in front of a mirror and practiced lifting my arm and moving it in a variety of gestures and positions. Now, I know how my shoulder looks when I move it in any particular way. I continued to practice those moves so that when I'm on stage, no one suspects that I have this problem, and I am able to camouflage it successfully. But make no mistake; it's a camouflage. It's amazing what the mind and will can do if you want something badly enough.

Certainly, one of the most vexing symptoms of the radical was the constant aggravation of fluid from my lungs. Before I was under anesthesia, there wasn't a thing wrong with me except the cancer on my face. Other than that, I was a perfect physical specimen.

But when I woke up, I was so full of phlegm that I thought I'd never get rid of it. It was awful. I suspect being in that cold recovery room for ten hours gave me the infection.

I gradually got rid of most of it, but for years, almost to this day, I didn't know when, absolutely out the blue, some phlegm would come up from my chest as an aftereffect of the operation.

I developed a fear that this phlegm would suddenly appear while I was singing, and worried that it would ruin the tone of my voice until I could expel it. After all, who can stop in the middle of a performance to get rid of phlegm? I never said anything to anyone about it, but it plagued me.

The other thing that happened, which no one bothered to warn me about, concerned my ear. For years I thought I was crazy because when I ate, the skin under my ear would water. I never said anything about it because I thought if I told anyone my ear was salivating, they would think I had lost my mind.

It wasn't anything another person would notice, but I could feel it. I would put my hand under my ear and pull it down, and sure enough, it would be wet. This went on for fifteen years. Then one day, someone who'd had the same operation told me his doctor had warned him it might happen. When the tiny salivary glands get disturbed, they can get loose and come out into the scar. I said, "Thank you so much. I'm so delighted to hear that because I've been experiencing it for years and I thought I was balmy."

It was unfortunate that I had a doctor with an attitude problem, not to mention an inflated ego. I base my conclusion on the fact that he wouldn't allow me to have my own doctor present for the radical, wanting it to be his "show." However, I wasn't there to be entertained.

Even his staff had adopted his arrogant attitude. After several weeks of recovery in Memphis, I flew back to New York for the doctor to have a look at me. I walked into his offices and told the nurse that I'd had an awful time trying to find this location.

She replied, "Well, you'd better learn where it is because from now until the end of your life, you will be coming to this office."

At that point I said to myself, *Oh yeah? Not here, sister. You can just bet that I won't be coming back here.* And I never did.

Later, I learned that Dr. Frizell had been relieved of his position at Sloane Kettering and moved to another state a short time after my operation. I have always thought, somewhere in the back of my mind, that perhaps he had done something very wrong to me.

When it came time for me to go home to Memphis, my husband's brother, Martin Condon, sent the Snuff Company jet to get me. I went directly from the hospital to the airport and made the trip home with no problems at all. I will be everlastingly grateful to Martin for that flight home. I did not want to get on a commercial flight all bandaged up and looking like I did, with two tubes in my throat for drainage.

When I got home, I went straight into bed. I had to sleep sitting up for one whole year, unable to lie down or turn my head or sleep on my stomach, which was the way I normally slept.

However, my children again rallied around me. Of course they were curious about how I would look and because I kept nothing from them, they knew basically what to expect. I brought them all up to my bedroom where I removed the bandages, pulled back my hair and showed them everything. I explained exactly what had been done and reassured them, still shaken by the death of their father seven months earlier that their mother was going to be just fine. And amazingly, I still am.

At the outset of this new start for me, I adopted the attitude that if people were going to like me, they would like me as I am. So a couple of months after the operation, when my friend, Arthur Spitzer, wanted to give a party for me in Los Angeles, I decided to go. That trip was sort of an ice-breaker for me, and gave me the courage to go out and do other things.

After the radical, I thought I was pretty terrible looking, so to cover the scar on my cheek, one doctor gave me a silk, flesh-colored patch with adhesive on one side. I began to wear this big patch on my cheek, which covered the scars and was a sort of mask to hide behind. I even became very comfortable with it.

At that time, Hathaway Shirts had a major ad campaign featuring a man with a black patch over one eye. He did a lot of TV commercials showing off their shirts while wearing this eye patch. I began to feel like the girl with the patch over her cheek. It was something I wore for about a year, until I had more operations to take away some of the scars on my face. I even performed with the patch, which didn't seem to bother anyone.

Husband #4: Harry Bergtholdt

In November, 1969, I was working in the Maisonette Room in New York and my friend, Paul Willis, was going to take us out to dinner on Saturday evening before my first show at 8:30. "Us" included Aunt Ann, my son, Billy, now about twelve years old, and me.

Paul's friend, Harry Bergtholdt, was in Washington, D.C., and called to say he was coming to New York and would like to take Paul to dinner on Saturday night. Paul told Harry he had a date Saturday night, and Harry said he would be glad to take both Paul and his date out to dinner. So Paul agreed and announced that his date would be Marguerite Piazza.

Harry didn't believe him. He said, "Paul, you've been talking about her for years, but you've never produced her. I certainly would like to meet her, if you can produce her this time."

Paul replied, "Just meet me at the St. Regis Hotel at 6:30 p.m." Harry thought that was a little early for a Saturday night in New York City, but Paul explained that I had to do my show at 8:30, so we would have to eat early.

Harry came to the St. Regis, expecting not to see Marguerite Piazza, but instead, Paul Willis with his girlfriend, Arlene. When he walked into the lobby, the first thing he saw were the posters advertising Marguerite Piazza, who was appearing in the Maisonette Room. Now, he thought, "By gosh, maybe he really does know her."

Sure enough, Paul brought him up to my suite. My son, Billy, let him in and then Aunt Ann and I walked out to meet Harry. There was an immediate attraction--Harry liked what he saw and I liked what I saw.

We went to "21" for dinner and Harry sat next to me, with Paul Willis on the other side. We talked all through dinner and had a wonderful time. After dinner, they escorted me back up to my suite and then left to get a seat for the first show.

Billy sat with them during the show and after it was over, said, "Excuse me, I have to go backstage to get my mother and take her back upstairs now." Billy escorted me upstairs, and the others followed shortly afterwards.

I got changed and cleaned up a bit and went out to join them in the living room. As soon as I sat down, Harry immediately sat down next to me. Paul did not like that at all, and said, "Harry, why don't you fix Marguerite a soft drink."

As soon as he got up, Paul came over and sat down next to me so Harry couldn't. He was actually jealous, which surprised me because I had no plans for a relationship with him. He was a dear friend, but beyond that, there was no interest on my part.

Finally, Harry and Paul were getting ready to leave, and I said, "I hope you'll stay for the second show," to which Harry said, "We'd love to."

But Paul said, "No, we're going home. Harry and I are playing golf early tomorrow morning and we have to get some rest." And because Harry had arrived with Paul, he had to leave, too.

A few months earlier, I had been dating a man from California. He came to see my show and stayed until two o'clock in the morning talking to me. Aunt Ann had stayed up with us because he was a great conversationalist. Finally, he got tired and left.

When Aunt Ann closed the door behind my friend, she turned to me and said, "You don't need that again, Marguerite. He's a playboy. And if there's anything you don't need, it's a playboy." But when

Harry left, she closed the door behind him, turned to me and said, "Now that's a man."

The next day was Sunday, and it snowed. It was late November and I waited all day for Harry to call me. Meanwhile, Harry was sitting in his hotel room doing paperwork and wondering whether or not to call me. As the snow continued to fall, he decided, *If I call her today, I'll be just like every other man who is going to call her. But if I don't call her, she'll remember it and she'll remember me.*

So he didn't call, but returned to California without saying goodbye. And he was right. I was upset, and I surely did remember him.

For Christmas, just a few weeks away, he sent me two dozen red roses, telling himself, *If she's interested, she'll write a thank you note.* And I did.

I also enclosed my itinerary for the next month. He found his way to one of the engagements on the list and eventually came to see me in Memphis. I had all the children downstairs, dressed in their finery to say hello before we went out to dinner. And so began my romance with Harry Bergtholdt. It was about nine months later that I married him.

Before we got married, I wanted to make sure Harry had some idea of what he was getting himself into. After my operation in 1969, I really didn't know how long I would live, or if I would live. So I asked my lawyer, Charlie Davis, if I could afford to buy a new mink coat. And he said "Yes Sweetnin', you sure can. You go get yourself a new mink coat." So, I went to New York and got carried away. I bought five fur coats!

Before I met Harry, I met a doctor in Florida who was quite smitten with me. He decided to visit me in Memphis and spent two days here. The first day, we went out to lunch and when we returned, there in the entry hall of my big house was this huge box. It looked almost like a coffin. But I knew exactly what it was and I said, "Oh, my coats have arrived!" He said "Coats?" And I said, "Yes, lets open them up. I want to show them to you."

I opened the box and started to pull out fur coats. One was a French dyed purple broadtail with purple fox trim and a big purple fox muff to match. I think it was the first one of that kind of thing in the United States and it was gorgeous. With every fur coat I pulled out, this man's face got longer and longer. He just could not fathom it at all. We went out to dinner that night, but the next morning, he was on the first plane out of Memphis. A few days later I received a letter saying that I had been delightful and he was glad to see me, but that I was much too extravagant for him.

So when I met Harry, I said to him, "Before I get too deeply involved with you, I want you to know that I am extravagant at times. For instance, my lawyer said that I could buy a mink coat, so I went to New York and I bought five fur coats. Now, what do you think about that?" He swallowed hard, looked at me and said, "Well, you must have needed them." Of course, he was thinking, she won't need another fur coat for years and he was right!

We had a huge wedding so I could introduce him to all my friends in Memphis. No one knew him because he was from San Francisco, so the weekend leading up to the wedding was a series of major events.

On Friday night in New York City, I received a great honor from the American Cancer Society. I became the National Crusade Chairman for 1971. I brought all my children to New York for the event, and my three daughters sang one number with me. Harry was there and we took over several rooms at the Waldorf Astoria. The event was in the Grand Ballroom, and I performed for thirty minutes at the end of the ceremony.

The next day, when we were going to the airport, Harry said he realized for the first time just what a big family he was inheriting, since it took two limousines to get us all there. That was Saturday.

In addition to the bride and groom, there were fifty out-of-town guests arriving in Memphis on Saturday, and we had friends and various people who worked for us meeting our guests at the airport and taking them to hotels. Although I was the bride, I gave the rehearsal dinner for the out-of-town guests and a few friends at the Memphis Country Club Saturday night.

On Sunday, my friend, Mary Arnette Tagg, had all of my out-of-town guests for brunch which was an enormous help. The wedding was at four o'clock in the afternoon in my home on Central Avenue, and only the out-of-towners, family members and a few friends attended the ceremony.

The wedding had a Russian theme. I collect cookbooks and found a wonderful picture of a painting in my Russian cookbook. I thought the headdresses were fantastic and the dresses were lovely, so I had a yellow and gold mid-calf length dress made, as well as gold boots and a gold Cossack hat embroidered with pearls and a fringe of crystal beads.

My hair was tucked under this hat with only a few little curls showing around my face and the girls wore tiara-shaped headdresses covered with gold lace. In New York the day before the wedding, I had gone to the area where all the hat shops were, and bought the materials and bodies for those headdresses. There were three milliners in Memphis who worked through the night to finish them for the wedding.

I had lined the main staircase in my house with yellow mums, and my children, my one bridesmaid, and I all marched down the stairs and proceeded through the front entrance hall to the living room, where we were married by a Justice of the Peace.

I was very excited to have a husband again. It seemed that throughout my life, I had always been married. Despite divorce and being widowed twice, I had never gone more than 2 years without a husband. To me, marriage felt like the most natural state. I felt I needed a father figure my growing children. And I also thought, as a successful business man, he would be a great help to me.

After the ceremony, we all had a little glass of champagne before everyone left to go to the Memphis Hunt and Polo Club for the reception at 5 p.m. I stood in a receiving line for several hours while everyone enjoyed the orchestra and a buffet dinner for four hundred people.

Few people realized it, but I suffered during that wedding. Boots had just appeared on the fashion scene in a big way, and I had thought I was very clever to have had gold lame boots made for me, my daughters, and my one bridesmaid.

But those boots caused me an awful lot of grief. It was years later when I discovered the cause. I had ordered a medium and received a narrow, but I put them on and didn't even think about it. I stood in those tight boots, receiving all those people for hours, and then danced in them.

By the time we got home, it was after 10 p.m., and when Mildred, my maid, pulled those boots off me, I felt as if she were unbinding my feet. The pain of blood rushing back into my feet felt as if someone were holding them in a fire. The tears just rolled down my face, even though I don't usually show when I'm in pain.

Mildred held my feet very tightly as I screamed, "Please don't let go." We put my feet in cold water, then hot water, but nothing helped. Fortunately, a doctor had followed the party to our home, and he gave me a pain pill. After about twenty minutes, it started to work.

Poor Harry stood over me on our wedding night, along with Monsignor Kearney, two maids and a doctor, watching and not being able to do anything to help.

Meanwhile, the group of friends that had come back to the house had a spaghetti supper without me and the party was still raging on downstairs at two o'clock in the morning.

I finally called down on the intercom and told them to get out and go home. I needed to get some sleep. I had to get up at 5 a.m. to dress and get to the airport to catch a plane. We had hitched a ride on the Snuff Company jet back to New York and had to be there for takeoff at 7 a.m. In New York, we caught a plane to Portugal for our honeymoon. And that, let me tell you, was a big weekend!

Working with The American Cancer Society

When I became the National Crusade Chairman for the American Cancer Society, I gave them one entire year of my life. I traveled throughout 1971 to 27 cities around the country, where I would speak and then sing to raise both money and awareness for the Cancer Society. This was the first year of my marriage to Harry.

While I was traveling, Harry was still living in San Francisco and traveling on business and then seeing me every once in a while. He commuted from San Francisco to Memphis when I was home for a weekend, which was very difficult, not to mention expensive.

My manager, Raymond Katz, advised me not to work with the American Cancer Society and told me not to let anyone know that I had cancer. He said it would be considered a stigma and would hurt my career.

I must say, he was correct that, at that time, it was a stigma. But it was something I felt I had to do, anyway. The information I was giving out to thousands of people on a daily basis that year was life-saving information. To teach people about the seven warning signals, to recognize them and take themselves to the doctor, rather than hoping they would go away, was very important to me.

I believe that information and education are the most important things you can give to another human being. With information, people can help themselves and hopefully prevent disaster, rather than having to try to cure it after the fact.

Cancer in the 1960's was almost as frightening as the AIDS virus in the 1980's, and people are finally waking up to the importance of information and education.

Although I have no regrets, working with the American Cancer Society was not good for my career at that time. The tobacco companies, who produced more than just tobacco products, were quite upset with me. Although I had worked for them a lot, singing at conventions and special events, they now wanted no part of me. Things have changed quite a bit since then.

Regardless of these obstacles, there were many more positive experiences that kept me going. To launch my yearlong crusade, I was invited to the White House by my friend, President Nixon, who presented me with the National Award for Courage, given once a year by the American Cancer Society.

I brought my two youngest children, Marguerite and Anna-Becky, with me, who were ecstatic at the prospect of meeting the President of the United States. We waited a long time for the Surgeon General to arrive and escort us into the Oval Office. To our shock, the Surgeon General, who's predecessor had recently put the first warning label on packs of cigarettes and declared them to be deadly, came walking in with a cigarette in his hand, smoking like a fiend.

During that year, the American Cancer Society made a film about my fight with cancer called, "The Marguerite Piazza Story." It was aired on public television stations in every major city around the United States and shown as many as seven times in each city.

The Cancer Society also used it as a promotional film. There was a long version that could be shown on TV, as well as and a shortened version to be used at meetings across the country. They made a separate film of my speech at the White House when I received the award for courage.

When the film crew came to Memphis, I was doing a big, open-air concert at the Overton Park Shell and they filmed it. Around that time,

I thought it would be fun to include my daughters in my work, and we learned a routine around the songs, "Raindrops Keep Falling On My Head" (which was a huge hit at the time) and "April Showers."

Each of the girls had her own dance routine. But at the end, my youngest, Anna-Becky, who was only eight years old, finished it off with high kicks. She was just a little thing, but she had a lot of pizzazz. Everybody thought she was adorable, and the experience must have had an effect on her because she is the only one of my children pursuing a career on the stage. And she's great!

After I had that number especially arranged for the girls, we performed it in several places, one of which was Palm Beach at a benefit with Bob Hope. My friend, Mary Sanford, called me up and asked me to be the star of the Cancer Ball in Palm Beach in 1972 and I said I would be delighted. I would also bring my girls to do one number with me. It was all set.

Then, Mary ran into Bob Hope and asked him if he would come and do the show, too. Suddenly it wasn't the Marguerite Piazza show anymore; it was the Bob Hope Show *with* Marguerite Piazza. Bob also brought in Trini Lopez and his group, and at that point, we had a pretty long show scheduled.

During rehearsals, Bob heard me practicing with the girls. I flew Marguerite and Anna-Becky down from Memphis and Shirley from Washington D.C., where she was in school at Holton Arms. After the rehearsal, I received a request by way of a messenger that Mr. Hope would prefer we not sing "Raindrops Keep Falling On My Head" because he used it in his act. But I had spent a lot of money to bring those kids to Palm Beach and we were going to do our version of the song.

I sent word back saying I was very sorry, but that's the only number these girls do, and the only thing we had orchestrated, and I'd brought them a long distance to sing this one particular number and we were going to do it. And we did.

Bob Hope was the MC and introduced Trini Lopez, who stayed on for an hour. Already, that's a long show. When it came time to introduce me, Bob sent along a messenger to say that he was dressing and could not introduce me.

So I said, that's fine, he doesn't have to introduce me. I looked at Harry and said, "Come over here and say 'Ladies and gentlemen,

Marguerite Piazza' into the mike," which he did. Then I walked out and did my show, including "Raindrops" with the children. It was a big success.

At that point, there had been almost two hours of show, and the guests were hardly youngsters. They were beginning to get up and go home. But Bob went on and closed the show with his version of "Raindrops Go Skiing Down My Nose!"

Bob was mad at me for a little while, but he was a good guy and didn't stay angry for long.

Shortly after that when he came to Memphis to do a show at the Coliseum, I introduced him. He was a great friend of my dear friend, Paul Willis, so we always heard from Paul about what Bob and Dolores Hope were doing. Paul even took me to their house for a visit once during my early days in the business, and for years I received a Christmas card from the Hope's.

After all was said and done, my year with the American Cancer Society accomplished several things for me. Although my new marriage was so hectic, it approached "crazy," my work with the Cancer Society was something that I needed at that moment. For the first time in my life, I was actually feeling quite imperfect, so it meant a lot to me to be working so hard at something so worthwhile.

It was also very healing for me to be back in front of the public so soon after my operation. To be working again was more than just a relief; it was a saving grace.

More important, my career was no longer a shield behind which I could hide from my woes. This was the real me they were seeing and hearing, not just the glamorous image, but me, speaking from my heart and soul with the house lights up.

This was radically different for me, a time of real personal growth and new understanding about people and the world around me. Being of service through the American Cancer Society gave me a new perspective on life and I am grateful for it.

At the end of my year as National Crusade Chairman for the American Cancer Society, I attended their Annual Banquet and Awards Dinner in the Grand Ballroom of the Waldorf Astoria in New York.

Joan Crawford had been chosen to succeed me as Crusade Chairman for 1972. The dais consisted of five tiers of tables filled with the various doctors who were receiving awards for their accomplishments during the past year. Joan Crawford was seated not far from me and I could see she had a speech written in large letters so she could see it. Of course, I can't make fun of that because guess who needs big letters? I do.

The banquet went on and on and on as doctor after doctor received award after award. All those speeches took quite a long time. During the program, a waiter kept coming up to the dais with what we thought was a large glass of ice water for Miss Crawford. As it turns out, it wasn't water at all. It was straight vodka.

The last item on the program was for me to introduce Joan and hand her the reins for the following year. I gave her a wonderful introduction, saying how great an actress she was, and how beautiful she'd been on the screen, and how wonderful she was as a businesswoman, because of her work with Pepsi Cola at the time. Then, I introduced "Miss Joan Crawford."

When she stood up, you could tell she was having some difficulty with her balance. She made her way to the podium and opened her speech, but she could no longer see it. So she put it aside and said, "I don't know how she does it. You know she got another husband!"

Suddenly, I realized she was referring to me. Then she said "Harry, where are you?! Put the spotlight on Harry. Harry, stand up and take a bow." The spotlight found my husband in the audience and reluctantly, he stood up and took a bow.

Then she said, "And now, I want to thank the president of Pepsi Cola for coming here with me tonight. How about a great big hand for the president of Pepsi Cola." There was a round of applause for the president of Pepsi Cola.

Then she said, "And while I'm at it, I'd like you all to meet the chairman of the board of Pepsi Cola, who makes all this possible for me to do this." She called his name and said, "Stand up. Let everybody see you. How about a wonderful hand for the chairman of the board of Pepsi Cola." More applause.

By now, the MC realized that she was not in control. He had a big bouquet of yellow roses as he got up and said, "Joan, we want to thank you for being here tonight and we want to give you these lovely roses."

But she wasn't finished. Instead, she told him, "Sit down, I'm not through." She went on and on, and I don't even remember what she said after that point, but everyone knew she was smashed.

Eventually, the MC insisted, "Now, Joan, you've really been wonderful. Here are your roses and thank you very much everyone for coming" and he closed the night.

We were all terribly embarrassed as they whisked Joan Crawford out of that ballroom faster than you can imagine. Then we all went upstairs to the suite of the executive director of the Cancer Society. He was pacing around the room saying, "Oh, my word, what have we done? What are we going to do? We'll only be able to book her at lunch."

But they didn't book her at all. She made one short film for them to use on TV and that was the end of her year as National Crusade Chairman.

Second Cancer

I had been through a horrific experience with cancer. However, I learned a lot from that experience, which enabled me to help others. But when my attention was drawn to other things, I began slipping back into old habits. I allowed stress to take over again, and a second cancer developed. I believe it was God's way of giving me a nudge. There was something more I should be doing and this was a very big nudge to get my attention.

Fortunately, my second cancer was not related to the first, which probably would have meant certain death. Although I had spent a year traveling all over the United States telling people to watch for the seven warning signals of cancer, when my own warning signals were flashing, I ignored them. Eventually, I was bleeding so much; I had to go to the doctor.

The pap smear came up with cancer of the uterus and cervix and the doctors had to operate immediately. Since I'd had cancer before, I elected to go to a cancer specialist for the procedure. Dr. Jack Pigott, in Memphis, decided to give me radiation first. He said it would sear the cancer cells and contain them so there would be less chance of spillage during the operation.

Altogether, I had over seventy hours of radiation therapy. I was given a general anesthesia so doctors could put a "cage" inside me that would hold the two sticks of radium. When I came to, they wheeled me back down the hall to my room. There was a sign on the door that read: "DO NOT ENTER - RADIOACTIVE."

Soon after that, the doctor came down the hall with a little red cart containing the two sticks of radium and put them into the cage implanted in my body. He told me that I could have shots for pain every three hours, but I wanted to avoid the drugs as long as I could. I lasted for two days, but on the third day, the burning was so horrendous I finally gave way and had a shot. Later, I had one more.

I think radiation has to be the worst thing I have ever experienced in my entire life. I was made to lie flat. I couldn't turn from side to side, and I wasn't even allowed to have a pillow. I had to remain perfectly straight, perfectly flat and absolutely still. That, in itself, was difficult enough, but then this thing started to burn, getting worse and worse and worse until it was agony. No young nurses were ever allowed in my room to protect them from radiation, and anyone who might want to have children was kept out. I had an older lady for my nurse and even she stayed outside the door most of the time.

During the time I was receiving the treatment, Monsignor Kearney came to see me. He asked me if I would like to receive the Sacrament of the Sick, and I said yes. So, with Harry watching, he anointed me and said prayers over me. After he finished and left, I said to Harry, "Do you know what Monsignor did for me?"

He said, "He gave you the Sacrament of the Sick."

I said, "Yes. But do you know what that is?"

"No," he replied honestly.

I told Harry it was the Last Rites of the Church, and I thought he was going to have a fit. I had to explain that it's not only for the dying, but it can also help you get better. Monsignor Kearney actually gave me the Last Rites a total of three times; once before I had the first radical surgery and twice after that with the second cancer.

When they finally removed the radium and I tried to sit up on the side of the bed, I couldn't. I was as limp as a dishcloth. Someone had to hold me so I could sit up. I had never experienced such a degree of weakness, and it sent me into a deep depression. I cried a lot and I'm not one who is given to tears.

Feeling unable to console me, Harry suggested I go to New Orleans and let Aunt Ann and Aunt Frances take care of me for a while. When someone you love is taking care of you, it makes a huge difference. They see to everything and it's all done with love, unlike with someone you might hire.

Love truly makes the difference. I had to wait four to six weeks before the next operation, so I went to New Orleans to recuperate from the radiation.

One evening, a friend of my aunt's came over and said, "Don't worry about a thing, Marguerite. You're going to be all right. We're programming it!"

I said, "You're what?"

She repeated, "We're programming it." I had no idea what this woman was talking about. She proceeded to tell me that she was working on a Ph.D. in Psychic Phenomenon at Tulane University, and that she had studied all manner of disciplines. She was going to take a seminar the next day in something called Jose Silva's Mind Control, and she wanted me to go with her.

I said, "I don't know. I don't know anything about it." But she convinced me that it could be good for me.

I called Harry and asked him if he knew anything about Mind Control and told him about the woman and the seminar. He just said, "I sent you down there to rest, not go to class." But he then said he'd think about it, and called me early the next morning to say, "Go."

I was glad he'd changed his mind because I had already decided to do it the night before. After I attended an orientation lecture, I signed up for the course. It turned out to be the best thing I could have done for myself.

At 9 a.m., I was at a little place on Magazine Street, where I spent the whole day in classes. I was still very weak, but gradually, I started feeling a little better. In fact, one of the first things they told us to do was to repeat to ourselves "Every day in every way, I am getting better and better."

It sounds simple, but it brought me out of my depression and changed my outlook completely.

When I returned to Memphis, the doctor immediately noticed a change in me. I was a lot more positive in my thinking. He knew that this would help me get through the coming operation.

Doctors usually refer to it as "having the will to get better," and that's exactly what it is. I had the operation with an improved state of mind and sailed through it. The doctor performed a complete hysterectomy, removing my uterus, ovaries, cervix and even my appendix. He also told me I had an 80% chance of never hearing from the cancer again, which I found to be pretty good odds. The odds remained in my favor and I beat cancer a second time.

Because of the time frame, I was unable to complete that first Mind Control course in New Orleans, but later Harry and I and the children all took it in Memphis. It turned out to be a very practical course, taught in plain English. Throughout the years, we took other similar courses, which only reinforced and put names on principles I'd used unconsciously all of my life. Performing an entire opera or doing two shows a night for weeks on end is an amazing feat of physical, mental and emotional control. Looking back, it's clear that I couldn't have done it without having complete control of my focused mind.

Life with Harry Bergtholdt

Before moving to Memphis, Harry had lived in San Francisco and had been the Director of Distribution for Del Monte Corporation. In the late 1960's, he was promoted to president of Encinal Terminals, a worldwide shipping, warehousing and trucking concern owned by Del Monte. In addition to the massive job of moving all that product from the fields to the packing centers and out to the distribution channels, Harry also helped Del Monte acquire 13 different companies.

He loved business. Running numbers and looking at balance sheets was his greatest amusement. He was an excellent company man and loved the environment of a large corporation, especially one with such tremendous backing and industry prestige.

Harry was also accustomed to living in a city on the cutting edge of culture and thought. In the summer of 1971, we were still trying to decide if he would come to Memphis or if I would move myself and my six children to San Francisco. To help me decide, we rented a house in Pacific Heights and spent the month of August by the Bay. While we all had a great time, I took one look at the Haight-Ashbury scene and the drug culture and quickly whisked my impressionable teenagers and young children back to Memphis.

Following my retreat, Harry resigned from Del Monte and came to Memphis to be with me and start all over again. At that time, I owned a small trucking company, which Harry took over. He grew the business and began buying other companies, which is what he had done at Del Monte. But this time, he didn't have the resources of a large corporation. He was taking a risk and banking on himself and on me. He had been so successful in the corporate world, I just assumed he would do the same as an entrepreneur.

Moving from San Francisco to Memphis in 1971 would be a tough transition for anyone. San Francisco is a temperate coastal climate that never gets too hot or too cold. Memphis is in just the right spot to have four full-blown seasons. Fall is cool and wet with a stunning riot of color that rivals the Northeast. Winter can be bitterly cold, though there's usually more ice than snow. Early spring rains loosen the ground, which erupts into expansive emerald green lawns and floral blankets of spring color. But summer brought a heat and humidity that Harry was totally unprepared for. It was as if he'd moved to another planet where gravity was stronger and forcefully slowed the pace of life. In the beginning, it was a big drag on his physical body and on his personality.

Culturally, San Francisco and Memphis really were like different planets, especially at that time. People in Memphis spoke slowly and with a pronounced accent that marked you as a local or an outsider. Buying a drink in a restaurant had only been legal for two years, and conversations tended to be centered around local issues.

I was doing my best to have dinner parties and introduce Harry to all my friends, and he tried to fit in, but it was not easy. Harry had belonged to an exclusive men's social club in San Francisco called "The Family." They had ties to the Napa Valley, and Harry really enjoyed the California wines. Perhaps it was his frustration with his new home, or maybe he had a small problem that just became bigger under stress, but he soon began drinking more and more of his precious California wine.

He told himself he didn't have a problem with alcohol because he never drank hard liquor, only wine. But alcohol is alcohol, regardless of the package. One night after Harry really tied one on, something in me snapped. I had survived two alcoholic husbands and I vowed then and there that I would never put myself through that again.

The next day when he was sober, I had a little talk with Harry. I told him he had a choice: wine or me. He chose me. And from that moment on until he died, he never had another ounce of any kind of alcohol.

I could put up with a lot of faults, but out-of-control drinking was not one of them. I really have to give him credit for that. If I had a glass of wine or a beer on occasion, it didn't bother him at all. And when we had a big party (which we did a lot), Harry ordered all the liquor and wine, set up the bar and served everyone drinks with a smile on his face. His drink of choice became iced tea.

Golf was a special source of pleasure for Harry, as was the Memphis Country Club. Like me, when he was working, he would hunker down over a stack of papers and hardly came up for air. Business consumed his concentration, so spending a day outdoors in the park-like setting of a golf course was a much-needed release from his daily stress. I had no interest in playing, but I always encouraged him to go.

Harry was a brilliant idea person and was way ahead of his time. Unfortunately, being too early is often as unprofitable as being too late. He started business after business, from trucking companies to designer water, with varied success.

Harry got together with a group of doctors in Memphis and formed a company called Music Mountain Water. This was the 1970's in a fiscally conservative town with a huge aquifer of artesian well water just beneath the city. The thought of buying bottled water was still an uphill push, and Harry sold the business just before the bottled water craze took off.

He also had a labor supply company, which he sold too soon. Eventually, these ventures took a toll on our finances.

Despite his lack of business success, Harry had a big heart. It was one of his greatest assets, but it was also his biggest downfall. He loved the underdog, even though the underdog often bit him. He was intensely spiritual and constantly seeking answers to questions most mortals never even ask.

It was a quest that began with Transcendental Meditation and continued throughout the rest of his life. We took a lot of other courses and went to many lectures, almost all of which were Harry's idea. It was a journey I participated in fully and one that deeply affected some of my previous, long-held beliefs. It was also a road I might not have ventured down had it not been for Harry's curiosity.

The Catholic Church has been very good to me and I still consider myself a practicing Catholic. But as with all groups, there are certain aspects that work for you and some that don't.

I grew up with the idea that it was noble to deny yourself. The imagery of sackcloth and ashes is pervasive and controlling in Catholicism. This sort of personal denial manifested itself in insidious ways. When I went to the theater, I always felt I should enter quietly and sit in the back. My Jewish friend, Minn Katz, used to get mad at me for doing that. She would say, "You need to walk down that aisle with your head up and sit right in front where everyone can see you!"

And in fear and trembling, I did it. But I would not have done it by myself. She told me I needed more "chutzpah," or nerve, which was sorely lacking in my education. Fortunately, some of that comes with age and experience, whether you're Jewish or not.

Harry also had a son, Robert, from his previous marriage. The hippie culture in San Francisco made a big impression on him, and while many of his young contemporaries got lost in a drug-induced haze, Robert chose to go to India and study the great religions and philosophies of the East.

He spent two and a half years in Ceylon (which is now Sri Lanka) and Nepal. As a Buddhist lay monk, he lived in caves and hermitages while he studied and traveled with religious leaders of that region. While in a monastery in Kopang, Nepal, his health deteriorated so badly, he had to come home.

He flew out of New Delhi to Europe and then to New York, where he caught a Greyhound bus to Memphis. When he finally appeared on our doorstep in the Spring of 1973, he was very thin and looked quite bizarre, dressed in a long flowing Tibetan shirt tied at the waist with a colorful belt. His Nepalese pants were about six inches too short because the Nepalese maker had never seen a man who was six foot four inches tall. His boots were woven with brightly colored Buddhist symbols and he was carrying a small backpack, which contained all his worldly possessions.

Becky answered the door and with eyes the size of saucers gasped, "Oh, my God!"

Robert said simply, "I'm Harry Bergtholdt's son," to which poor Becky could only exclaim, "What?!"

206

Robert repeated it and Becky closed the door, leaving Robert outside, and ran down the hallway to summon Harry, who hadn't seen his son since 1969.

But when they saw each other, all the old conflicts melted away. We took Robert into our home and into our hearts. The children were especially impressed with his amazing yoga abilities. They thought anyone who could put both legs behind his head was a new brother worth having! And that's what he's been ever since.

St. Jude Children's Research Hospital

In 1962, Danny Thomas saw his dream become a reality as the St. Jude Children's Research Hospital opened its doors for the first time. With the help of a group of business leaders from Memphis, he managed to raise the funds to get it built. Then came the daunting task of raising the money to keep it running. For this, Danny turned to fellow Americans of Arabic-speaking heritage.

Believing deeply that Arabic-speaking Americans should, as a group, thank the United States for the gifts of freedom given their parents, he also felt supporting St. Jude would be a noble way of honoring his immigrant forefathers who had come to America. Danny's request struck a responsive chord. In 1957, 100 representatives of the Arab-American community met in Chicago to form ALSAC (The American Lebanese Syrian Associated Charities) with a sole purpose of raising funds to support St. Jude Children's Research Hospital.

In the beginning, Danny and the local business leaders organized a fundraiser in Memphis called, "The Shower of Stars." Lots of famous Hollywood stars came to Memphis to do the show, and I performed, too. But the show only lasted two years.

I was a supporter of the hospital from the beginning through my friends Monsignor Kearney, Ed Barry and John Ford Canale. When the first star-shaped building was dedicated, I sang the "Star Spangled Banner."

That's when I met my friends, Margaret Ann and Dr. Eugene Murphy. Their eight-year old daughter, Margaret, was one of the first children to be cured at the hospital. She and another child spoke at the opening. They were living miracles and shining examples of what the doctors at St. Jude Hospital could do every day for the children of the world.

The Murphy family had been told that Margaret had a mass in her chest that was inoperable and, in their opinion, she had about two weeks to live. But they decided to treat her anyway. Today, Margaret is a nurse in the cancer unit at a hospital in their home town of Tupelo, Mississippi.

In 1975, I put together a new supper club act, and before opening at the Shamrock Hotel in Houston, I wanted a place to try it out. My booking agent at the time, Cy Rosenthal, said we should put on a ball and give the money we made to a charity. He said, "Pick a charity, Marguerite." So I picked St. Jude.

Harry and I engaged a hotel ballroom, the band, musicians and a conductor. Then we had invitations printed. My teenage son, Gregory, ran the sound and lights, and my friends, mostly from the Memphis Country Club, bought tickets. We were now in business.

The evening was so successful; we decided to do it again the following year. At that time, there had never been a gala for a charity in the city's history.

In April 2006, we presented my 31st Annual Marguerite Piazza Gala for St. Jude Hospital. After running the gala myself the first five years, we decided to elect a board of directors and a chairperson. These wonderful people have worked so hard to make the Gala a success and to help fund St. Jude's incredible work. They include John Ford Canale, Edmond D. Cicala, Joseph G. Costa, Donald L. Hutson, Fred P. Gattas, Sr., Bruce B. Hopkins, Robert L. Leatherman, Sandy Lewis and Geri McCormack.

We began to add more stellar performers to the bill, many of whom worked gratis. Some of our performers through the years have included Jim Nabors, Dihann Carroll, Tony Martin, Nancy Wilson of the Supremes, Carmen Cavallero, Mimi Hines, Connie Haines, Don Cornell, Kay Starr, Margaret Whiting, Jerry Vale, The Association, The Spinners, The Coasters and Gary U.S. Bonds, to name just a few.

Every year, we award the Marguerite Piazza Healing Rose to a person who has contributed outstanding service to the hospital. The Rose is a gorgeous, large pink porcelain piece created by the Edward Marshall Boehm Studio especially for the Marguerite Piazza Gala, and is not sold anywhere else.

I had no idea when I started this gala that it and the St. Jude Children's Research Hospital would become such an integral part of my life, but in fact, it has become just that! The Marguerite Piazza Gala for St. Jude is one of the longest running annual charity balls in America.

Losing Jimmy

There are many things in life that are impossible to prepare for. Children, for instance. They don't come with instructions. One day, they're just here. My son, Jimmy, was not very stable emotionally, possibly from a number of causes, rather than any single event. But he was always very high-strung and very self-willed.

Jimmy was an artist, studying painting in college. He would go to class to learn everything he wanted to know about a particular subject, and then leave and not go back to that class anymore. I had to insist that it was important for him to take his exams, but he'd protest, saying, "What for? I already know what I want to know from that class. I don't need anything more."

I had to say "But the school requires that for your grade, Jimmy."

"I don't need a grade," he would say.

When he went to look at schools on the West Coast, Harry took him to several and watched as Jimmy interviewed the dean. He wanted to know what the dean was going to present and if he was going to like it.

Jimmy had tremendous will, but he was emotionally immature and insecure. A doctor in Memphis once diagnosed him as schizophrenic and manic-depressive. He also had a destructive streak.

His father, Graves McDonald, had been emotionally weak, which perhaps contributed to his instability. Even when Jimmy was a child, we had to watch him because he was different from the other children.

Jimmy was even hospitalized once, the year before he died. The psychiatrist put him on drugs that turned out to be overwhelming, and when Jimmy came home, he walked around like an automaton. He realized that the drugs were not good for him, so he stopped taking them and came back to normalcy.

He was fine for about a year until suddenly, he went back into the depths of depression. I called the psychiatrist who had taken care of him before, but he was out of town. There was another doctor taking his calls, but Jimmy would have no part of him.

One afternoon, Jimmy came over to the house very upset, and Harry took him into his converted office in the carriage house and talked to him. Harry was always a spiritual seeker, and this time he tried age regression to probe what was happening inside Jimmy's mind, taking Jimmy back to when he was a child to see what might be bothering him.

Jimmy seemed to get rid of a few things that were on his mind and when he came out of it, he was sobbing. Harry put his arms around him and said, "I love you, Jimmy." Jimmy told Harry that he loved him, too.

Then, Harry asked Jimmy it he could tell Mama he loved her and he said, "Oh, yes." He ran across the back yard to the main house. I was in the kitchen when he threw his arms around me, kissed me and said, "Oh, I love you, Mama. I love you, Mama."

I hugged him and told him I loved him, too. I sat him down on the little stool in the kitchen and I patted his face and asked, "What's wrong Jimmy? Are you all right?"

"Yes," he said. "I'm all right now." I told him I was just fixing dinner and asked him to stay and eat a little bit, but he said, "I don't know."

"Marguerite and Anna-Becky are in the music room," I told him, and he went in there and kissed both his sisters and hugged them and told them he loved them. Then he went for a walk with Marguerite.

When he came back, he said, "I have to go." I pleaded with him to stay and told him he didn't have to go back to his apartment alone. But he refused to stay and insisted that he had to go.

But before he left, I said, "Come upstairs. I have some nice bandanas I bought. I know you like bandanas and I want to give you some." We went up and I brought a few dozen bandanas out of the closet. I picked out some colorful ones to give him and he snapped, "Mama, don't you understand, I can't see color now."

I didn't understand what he meant at the time, but the psychiatrist told me later that this was our clue that Jimmy was going to kill himself. He had already closed out color.

Today, however, I would like to tell anyone who has children or is around someone who is disturbed or depressed that when they refuse to see color, you must get help immediately.

Color was especially important in Jimmy's life because he was a painter. When he said that to me, he was saying he had already made up his mind to kill himself. Not knowing what to do, I picked out two bandanas that were beige with a black print on them. I said, "These have no color on them. Would you like to have these?" He grabbed them and said "All right!" To please me, he took them. Then I kissed him and he went out the door.

Once outside, Jimmy started to get into his car, but he walked around it and said, "I have a flat tire." He kicked the tire and came back inside. I sent Harry out to look at the car, but he said there was no flat. Jimmy had only wished it was flat so he would have an excuse to stay with us and not face what he was planning to do.

Then, he started the car. It worked and he drove down the driveway. That was the last time I ever saw him.

All this happened on a Saturday. On Sunday evening, Jimmy's girlfriend, Amy, called me to ask if I knew where Jimmy was. I told her I had been calling his apartment, but never getting an answer. We had no idea that Jimmy was dead, having killed himself about two o'clock that afternoon.

We learned this from the lady in the apartment next door, who told us that Jimmy had the door open and was playing the piano. He had come over to her and said, "I hope I don't disturb you."

The neighbor replied, "Oh, no, Jimmy. I like to hear you play the piano. Just leave the door open. I like to listen."

She said he was dressed very nicely in his gray turtleneck sweater and jeans. Then he went back to his apartment, leaving the door slightly ajar so someone could find him. She heard the shot, but her apartment faced the street and she thought at the time it was the sound of a car backfiring.

Earlier on Sunday, my decorator friend, Roy Monday, had come to see me. He was very upset about a small cancer that the doctors had discovered on his ear. I spent the afternoon with Roy, but I really couldn't do anything for him and I finally took him home about five o'clock.

That's when I started calling Jimmy, but there was no answer. Amy had come home from work and gone to his apartment building, but the doorman wouldn't let her in. She explained that she couldn't get her boyfriend on the phone and wanted to go up and see him, but he refused to let her in without a key.

Monday morning, I started calling again. I had asked Amy to call and let me know Jimmy was OK if she found him, but I hadn't heard from her.

At noon, Amy went back to his apartment and slipped inside the door behind a man who was going in. She went upstairs, found the door slightly open and discovered Jimmy seated on the floor, leaning against the wall of his bedroom. He had put the barrel of a shotgun in his mouth and pulled the trigger.

The sight was such a shock to her that she ran out, got into her car, and drove straight over to my house. It was about noon, and a friend had come over to tell me about her trip to Ireland.

We were sitting in the library looking at pictures when Amy's little Volkswagen came racing up the driveway. I knew right then something was very wrong and excused myself. I ran through the back hall to the kitchen door as Amy was getting out of her car. She came running towards me and I shouted, "Amy, it's Jimmy isn't it?"

She shook her head. She was so hysterical that she couldn't form words.

I said, "Amy, he's sick?" And she shook her head, no.

I said, "He's dead." She nodded her head, yes. She was still unable to speak, but I kept saying, "Are you sure? Are you sure?" She just kept nodding her head, a stricken look on her face.

Rebecca was there and my teenage daughter, Marguerite, had come home from school for lunch. I sent my friend across the street to the school to get Anna-Becky, and then called Monsignor Kearney and asked him to go to Jimmy. He went immediately.

Then I called my doctor, Mac DeMere, and said, "I want you to go see Jimmy. I think he's dead." He rushed right over there, and the two men found the body and later came to see me, confirming that Jimmy was dead.

No one told me how Jimmy had done it, but Mac said to me, "He couldn't have suffered, Marguerite. The way he did it, death was instantaneous." When the funeral people came to get him, I knew he'd shot himself, but I didn't know exactly what he'd done, so I got clothes and shoes and everything out for them to dress him nicely.

Unfortunately, I found out how he died by reading it in the papers the next day. No one could bear to tell me.

Jimmy's death was broadcast on national TV, and reporters and photographers surrounded my house for days. The way they announced the story on TV, a lot of people just heard my name and the word "suicide." Soon people from around the country started calling to see if I was still alive.

My friend, Bud Dudley, gave the homily for Jimmy's funeral, which was perfectly beautiful, and I will always be grateful to him for that.

About a year after Jimmy's death, I decided to go through all his belongings. They had been stored in my basement. I finally felt I could throw out or give away what I didn't want to keep.

There were things like sheets, clothes, a lampshade, books, etc. that had dark blood stains and a gray, dried matter all over them. I began to clean some of the things that looked salvageable when suddenly I realized I was throwing parts of my son into the garbage. I was so upset by the thought, I took what I could and I buried it. But his belongings should never have been brought to me in that condition.

I have been through many difficult experiences in my life, but my son's suicide hit me very hard. It was something I didn't know how to deal with. Who was to blame? Was there anything I could have done to prevent it? How could he have done such a thing? Was he afraid? There was so much I didn't know.

I wanted to understand. I wanted to know why. My family and friends could console me, but no one had any satisfying answers to any of my questions. And my interest in the mind, the spirit and the powers that exist in our subconscious minds arose once again. I read more books and attended more classes, but nothing could fill the hole in my heart. Losing a child is especially tragic. Though it's never easy, we sort of expect our parents to die first. But losing a child, especially to suicide, was almost beyond my comprehension. My only consolation is knowing in my heart that Jimmy is in a better place. He suffered so in life. But now, I believe he's in peace.

Yet Another Challenge

In the late 1970's, I was asked to do a pilot for a game show with the promise that if it went well and was picked up by a network, I would be on the permanent panel. I went to California and we spent an entire evening rehearsing this show. We all sat around a table on the set, looking toward one end where the man who was running the game was sitting.

There was a big light overhead with a Tiffany-type shade that reflected light right into my eyes. It bothered me the whole three or four hours we sat there, but we were busy learning and playing the game, and I didn't pay it a whole lot of mind.

After we finished, we went out to eat and afterward, I went over to my friend Ann Hamilton's house. Her son is the actor, George Hamilton. Ann had a very interesting group of artists and designers assembled at her house and we stayed up until 2 or 3 in the morning. I finally went back to my hotel and went to bed.

At 7 a.m., I woke up with a horrible pain. It was as though someone had poured ground glass in my eyes. I couldn't understand it. I had some salt, so I made a warm saline solution and bathed my eyes, but it didn't help.

Finally, I called Gail, Ray Katz' secretary, and said, "I'm in such pain and I don't know what's wrong with me. Please come right away."

By the time she arrived, I couldn't see anything. I was just lying on the bed, writhing with pain. She called several eye doctors and tried to get one to come to my hotel. But when no one in L.A. would come, she decided to take me to an eye doctor in Beverly Hills.

I couldn't stand any light at all, so I held a damp washcloth over my eyes while she put my dress on me. We didn't even bother with underwear. We got the dress on and some shoes and Gail led me to her car, put me in it, drove me to the doctor's office and led me like a blind person into the elevator and up to his office.

When the doctor looked into my eyes, he said, "Your eyeballs are terribly burned. You must have been looking into a light." I told him about the glass over the light fixture the night before and he said that was like trying to start a fire with the sun and a magnifying glass. The glass had reflected the heat and burned my eyes.

The doctor put drops in my eyes, then bandaged them and told me I'd have to stay with someone, as I was to leave the bandages on for two days. I went to Raymond's mother, Minn Katz, who took excellent care of me. It's amazing how something as simple as trying to eat by lifting a spoon to your mouth, when you can't see where it's going, is really an achievement.

I marvel at people who are really blind and their ability to get around and do things for themselves. Needless to say, I didn't make the game show.

Retirement

In the early 1980's, I thought I would take time off from my career. I had been working virtually nonstop, traveling and singing, from the time I was eighteen years old. I used to think I had missed something by not being a housewife and stay-at-home mom. So many of my women friends didn't work outside the home, and I decided one day I'd like to stay home for awhile. I wanted to cook and spend time with my husband and children, who were beginning to have children of their own.

I went into semi-retirement. I was still performing, but I was more of a regional performer and only doing concerts. There would be no more two-week jobs out of town. And I was beginning to have a good time.

I still wanted to travel, but on my own time and to places I wanted to see. In October of 1987, my daughter-in-law, Mia, and I went to the Soviet Union. It was a special trip organized by the Blue Army, a Roman Catholic group, the Army of the Blessed Virgin. 1987 was the seventieth anniversary of the October Revolution, and there were a lot of celebrations commemorating it. But our project was to return an important icon that had belonged to the Russian Orthodox Church to celebrate the 1000 years of Christianity in Russia.

The entire trip was really quite amazing. I don't think it would even have been possible just two years before, and it was not yet as free and open as it is today. But we were allowed to visit the Monastery at Zagorsk and attend mass there, intermingling with the Soviet people. That was really something in 1987!

However, there were several disappointments during our trip. The icon was to be gifted at a great ceremony. This had been planned before we left the United States and I was to sing. But the lines of communication went so haywire once we were in the Soviet Union, the ceremony never got off the ground.

A government official tried to explain that the monastery where the ceremony was to take place was being renovated and was not available. Therefore, two representatives from our group took the icon and presented it to church officials without any ceremony. One minute we had it, and the next, it was just gone. And I was not allowed to sing.

J. Rand McNally, Jr., the nuclear physicist, was also in our little group. He had made plans to meet with a group of Soviet scientists and the Soviet press, including Soviet Life Magazine and national TV. He was told everything was in place, but it never cleared in the USSR. However, he did communicate with Andrei Sakharov and decided that he would plan his own face to face meeting with his fellow scientist. And he did just that.

Mia and I were the first to see Rand when he got back and he was so excited. I bought him a whiskey and he told us the whole story. When he left our hotel and got into a taxi, he discovered he was being followed, apparently by the KGB. This meeting was very important to him and he didn't want anything to stop him, so he convinced this taxi driver to take part in a wild chase through the streets of Moscow, losing their tail and assuring his clandestine meeting with Sakharov.

When he arrived at the apartment, Sakharov's wife and scientist Elena Bonner, answered the door and asked him to come in and have some tea. I believe they were discussing the possibilities of surviving a nuclear winter. Both agreed that more testing would have to be conducted and even discussed where this testing should take place. McNally said that Sakharov suggested a particular place in the U.S. because of its greater security. He talked about specifics of American security as though they were general knowledge, but they were things that not even McNally knew, which surprised him.

We were in the Soviet Union for a total of ten days, but it felt more like a month. They were really not equipped for tourism at that time. The hotels were uncomfortable, the food was barely edible, and in general things were frustrating and inconvenient.

However, the sites were magnificent. To see the incredible opulence and extravagance of the Czars, and to know how destitute the people were, reveals why they had a bloody revolution.

On the last day of our trip, we boarded the bus with our driver and tour guide, Ludmilla. The air in the bus was thick with tension. Some of us had trouble getting rid of all our rubles and some were worried we might be stopped because we were taking money out of the country. All were very anxious to get home and to be on American soil.

On the road leading out to the airport that day, we witnessed an awesome sight. About every ten feet was an armed soldier standing at attention. They were lined up one after another literally for miles. In all of the Soviet Union, this was the first time we had seen weapons. We had seen a lot of soldiers but never any guns.

We tried to ask our guides what this display was for, but they were very vague. It must have been for a visiting head of state or perhaps for Gorbachev. It didn't really scare us, but in our present state of mind, it was certainly intimidating.

Now, the atmosphere in the bus was so thick you could cut it with a knife. And since I had been denied the opportunity to sing for the church, I stood up on that bus and began to sing "God Bless America." I just thought we needed it. And when I finished, there wasn't a dry eye on that bus, including those of our driver and Ludmilla.

I saw, at that moment, the end of Communism. Ludmilla, who had been extremely pro-Soviet up to this point and practically looked down her nose at us, had tears in her eyes. She wasn't an American. But she was a human being. She understood what we felt.

The theory of Communism looks great on paper, but the one thing it ignores is humanity: our compassion, greed, hopes, fears, personal opinions and ideas. The only way it could possibly work would be if everyone in the community were Christ-like. I would never have put such a rapid time frame on it, but I knew right then that Communism was not long for this world.

Singing "God Bless America" like that was not the first time I've done such a thing. A few years earlier, I was with an international group of people who plan world tours. We were in Spain, and my friend, Tiru Irani, who was the organizer of this trip, had purchased a little toy. It was stick-like, and attached to the end were several strings with little prickly steel balls at the ends.

The toy looked like a small reproduction of a medieval weapon. My friend had made a big joke about how he was going to hang it on the wall of his office and point to it when his secretary didn't do something right, but two Spanish soldiers were not smiling when they stopped him before boarding the plane. "Why do you want this?" they asked.

Seeing that they were giving him a little bit of a hard time, I thought it would be funny to have a picture of this scene and pulled out my camera and snapped the shutter.

Immediately, two big men came running over to me, grabbed my camera, picked me up by the arms and carried me off. They took me to a little room, pushed me in and locked the door. This all happened so fast I couldn't think. The soldiers had been screaming at me in Spanish, which I couldn't understand, and suddenly I was locked up. The plane was boarding for our trip home and I had no idea what was going to happen to me.

What I didn't know was that you are not allowed to take a picture of a soldier without his permission. Fortunately for me, the vice-president of Iberian Airlines, which we were traveling on, was in our party. He went straight to the head of the airport, who was a woman, and got them to release me.

Those two old soldiers had served under General Franco, and if he'd still been in power, no one could have gotten me out. They took my film, but they did return my camera. As soon as we were in the air and the seat belt sign went off, I stood up and sang, "God Bless America," and everybody cheered.

Harry's Death

One morning in 1998, I woke up, looked at Harry and noticed he was yellow and jaundiced. We got dressed and rushed to a doctor, who ran a battery of tests. The prognosis was grim. Harry had cancer of the pancreas, and the doctor told him he had 30-90 days to live. But they didn't know Harry and they didn't know me.

We went for a second opinion, but the diagnosis was still pancreatic cancer. However, this doctor told us he didn't want to give us false hope, but it was possible that Harry had *islet cell carcinoma of the pancreas*, a very rare form of pancreatic cancer. If this was the case, he might have a chance to live.

He also told us there was an experimental serum in development, but he wasn't sure he could get access to it. I told him I gave a year of my life to the American Cancer Society and he should make a few calls to see if there was anything anybody could do. As it turned out,

218

Harry had all the right conditions for the experiment, and we got the serum.

The serum had to be injected, and for three years, Harry gave himself three shots a day, usually in the belly. We had to pay for those shots ourselves, because they were not covered by insurance. But they were working. The cancer got smaller and more compact, but it never went away entirely.

Harry's diet was another major factor in his remission. My daughter, Marguerite, gave him Dr. Barry Sears' book, *The Zone Diet*, which had just come out. In the same way he had given up alcohol and never looked back, Harry gave up his beloved ice cream and cookies. He went on the most austere form of the diet and stayed on it until the last year of his life. He believed it was a major factor in extending his life.

Eventually, the serum was improved, and for two more years, Harry gave himself two shots a day. Finally, they developed a timed-release version, which the doctor gave him once a month for another year. I guess it had finally been approved because Medicare picked up the tab for the last year.

But suddenly, the serum stopped working and the cancer began to grow. It spread to his liver, and he was very sick for about six months. He used to say to me, "I'm losing my concentration."

I took care of Harry for five years. It wasn't bad in the beginning, but when he took a turn for the worse, we got a hospital bed at home. I slept in the bed next to him and even walked him to the bathroom in the middle of the night. But the weaker he got, the heavier he became and I didn't have the strength to handle him anymore.

He spent ten days in Baptist Hospital while I looked for a place that could care for him and finally arranged for him to go to the St. Peter Villa, where he received excellent care.

One day, back when the cancer was still in remission, I told Harry he should get out of the house and play golf. His answer to me was that his only interest now was preparing himself for the next dimension.

For over thirty years, Harry got up every morning, showered, dressed and made his way to a big comfortable chair where he spent at least one hour meditating. I think meditation did for Harry what singing did for me. It made him feel good. It was a stress reliever. And it helped him get through his own tough times.

The night before he died, my friend, Margaret Ann Murphy, had come up from her home in Tupelo, Mississippi to be with me. We went to visit Harry and were trying to be cheerful and talk with him. He was very weak and managed to whisper, "Margaret Ann, I'm so sorry. I can't talk."

We went home so he could rest and they called me at 7:05 a.m. the next morning to let me know he had passed on. That was in March, 2003. Just minutes before he died, he asked the nurses to help him sit up in a chair with both feet flat on the floor. They didn't know it, but that was the way he always sat during his meditation. He wanted to leave his body from that prayerful position.

When I got to St. Peter's, they had already placed him back in his bed. He looked so peaceful. I said to him, "You finally made it to the next dimension. I hope you're happy." When Harry died, my thoughts were not about myself. If anything, I was relieved. He had suffered in those last days and I truly believed he was ready to pass on. It was what he wanted and I had to just let him go.

Moving On

It's been a full life for me to this point, with no signs of stopping. Oh, there are a few things I'd like to go back and change, but there are an equal number of things (if not more) that I wouldn't have missed for the world. I have been on top of the world, higher than I ever dreamed I could go. I've had commercial success, a deeply passionate love, an amazing family and wonderful friends. But in the balance, experiencing cancer, divorce, the deaths of three husbands, my mother, my father and my son Jimmy has been more difficult than I could have imagined.

My work has truly been a salvation through all my trials and tribulations. Some of my friends say that the real Marguerite Piazza is the one on stage; that I function at a higher level of consciousness on the stage. All I know is that many of the happiest moments of my life have been when I was performing.

However, like the famous clown in the opera, *Pagliacci,* left alone on the stage to confess how he must act out his part wearing a big smile even though his heart is breaking, I have also taken solace on the stage.

No matter how you look at it, life for me has been about singing. Performing. Being before the public. This is the way I have lived my entire life and it is what I have enjoyed more than anything else in the world, except, of course, my children. They have always managed to be a grounding force for me and to remind me of what is really important in life.

But life has a funny way of changing. Just when I think I've got it all figured out, I find I have another lesson to learn. The body contracts and the mind expands.

There's an old joke: *Would you like to know how to make God laugh? Tell Him your plans!*

Right now, I find myself on yet another precipice. I have within me the young student with the fresh, open mind and heart, ready to absorb everything new. I have within me the polished performer of my craft. And I have within me the pearls of wisdom granted by a full life, ready to be shared with those who are seeking information from someone who's been down a road they wish to travel – or not travel. It is important for everyone, but especially for women, to honor their life experiences. Know that the world needs your gifts.

Alone once again, I find myself setting out on a new road, not knowing what's ahead for me. I have finally learned that how I feel about this leg of my journey through life is completely up to me. I have my faith in God and in myself. And all I can say is that the view from here is exhilarating.

House on Central Avenue

Marguerite with Richard Amberg and Kyle McDonald

Marguerite's Mother: Margaret Breland

Marguerite with Monsignor Kearney

PAGLIACCI HAS NOTHING ON ME!

Happy New Year

Christmas Card 1965

Marguerite with Face Patch, Denton Cooley

Paul Willis, Marguerite, Harry Bergtholdt

Marguerite and Harry at Wedding 1971

Marguerite with Danny Thomas

Marguerite with son Jimmy 1971

Marguerite with Harry 1989

Marguerite with Dominick Dunne 1991

Portrait by Avedon

Printed in the United States
79626LV00006B/119

9 781847 283948